BUYING A
MOTORBOAT
NEW OR SECOND-HAND

BUYING A
MOTORBOAT
NEW OR SECOND-HAND

BARRY PICKTHALL

ADLARD COLES NAUTICAL
LONDON

Published by Adlard Coles Nautical
an imprint of Bloomsbury Publishing Plc
50 Bedford Square, London, WC1B 3DP

www.adlardcoles.com

Copyright © Barry Pickthall 2012

First edition published 2012

ISBN 978 1 4081 5417 5

A CIP catalogue record for this book is available from the British Library.
This book is produced using paper that is made from wood grown in managed,
sustainable forests. It is natural, renewable and recyclable. The logging and
manufacturing processes conform to the environmental regulations of the
country of origin.

Typeset in Helvetica Neue LT Std
Designed by Kayleigh Reynolds/PPL Ltd
Illustrations by George Gray/PPL Ltd
Printed and bound in Spain by Graphy Cems

Contents

Introduction

There is something quite magical about motorboats. You can ski behind them, fish or dive from them, and use them to potter about on the river or cruise at speed from port to port. It is a pastime that the whole family can enjoy.

▶ Look before you leap

Buy the right boat for your needs and you will be a happy boat owner. Don't fall into the trap of allowing hearts to rule heads by falling in love with the first boat you see, and then regretting your purchase at leisure. This book provides a step-by-step guide to buying a boat, new or second-hand, it steers you around the hidden pitfalls, provides money-saving advice and helps you to select one that will give you years of enjoyment.

TIP
If you are buying through a dealer or from stock, check that the company operates a client account, and make payments directly to that account name.

That's all very well, but since buying a powerboat can be one of the biggest purchases you may make, it is prudent to know what you are doing – before going afloat. In the US, they have a slogan 'Get boat-smart from the start'.

It is certainly worthwhile enrolling the family in a sea school to learn not just the rudiments of getting a boat to go where you want it to go, but how to communicate, dock and navigate competently. These are essential skills and your choice of boat will be all the more informed once you are competent and confident enough to take her out for the day or weekend.

▼ Ten questions to ask yourself before signing the cheque:

1. Who will use the boat?
2. How will you use her?
3. How often will the boat be used?
4. Where will you operate her?
5. What is your budget?
6. What type of motorboat will best suit your temperament?
7. Which construction type should you opt for?
8. Where should you base her?
9. Should you opt for single or shared ownership?
10. Should you charter her?

1. Who will use the boat?

Just family, or will you have friends onboard? This can have a bearing on size and interior layout.

2. How will you use her?

- Water-skiing
- Fishing
- River cruising
- Coastal cruising
- Diving

3. How often will the boat be used?

Seasonally or year-round?

4. Where will you operate her?

- River/estuary
- Offshore
- Live-aboard

5. What is your budget?

Determine what you can afford, not just the purchase price but ongoing costs. These include:
- Fuel costs
- Mooring fees
- Insurance
- Registration fees
- Safety equipment
- Annual maintenance
- Instruction courses

6. What type of motorboat will best suit your temperament?

- Are you competitive by nature, or prefer to cruise at a leisurely pace.
- If you are a speed junkie, then fuel costs could temper your choice as far as size and power is concerned.
- For cruising offshore, seaworthiness, and protection from wind and spray will be priorities.
- If you are looking to base her inland, mooring availability could dictate overall length.

7. Which construction type should you opt for?

- Fibre-reinforced plastic
- Wood
- Aluminium
- Steel

8. Where should you base her?

- On a trailer at home
- Swinging mooring
- Trots
- Marina

9. Single or shared ownership?

- Fully owned
- Shared with family
- Shared with partner(s)
- Consortium

10. To buy or charter?

Divide the number of days that you anticipate using the boat by the annual budget. It may prove much cheaper to charter.

Hull types

What type of motorboat to buy? For many, there is a bewildering choice of shapes and sizes, some of them specific to the conditions and uses they will be put through. If you are interested in fishing on lakes or rivers then a stable, flat-bottomed boat will best serve your needs, but if waters are choppy or there is a coastal swell to counter then a boat designed to cut through the waves will be infinitely more comfortable. Hull forms are divided into two broad categories: displacement and planing.

Flat bottomed hulls

These provide the best performance in flat-water conditions and are also very stable, but slam badly in waves. They are favoured particularly as tenders, workboats and for fishing on inland waters. Their stability allows people to move freely around the boat when casting lines or nets. Some boats like the Cobia (opposite page) are fitted with an electric outboard on the bow for quiet, low speed trolling.

The specialist ski boat has become highly developed with a V bow and flat run aft to minimise wake, central fins to help maintain a steady straight line course, and an inboard engine set in the middle of the boat to provide the right balance. The latest designs have the tow-rope attached to an overhead bar also set amidships which further improves balance.

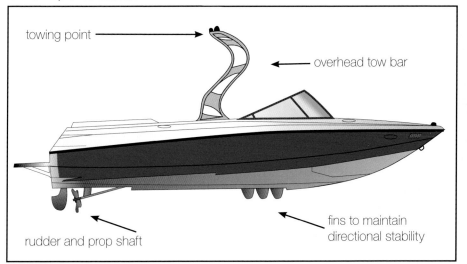

towing point

overhead tow bar

rudder and prop shaft

fins to maintain directional stability

A tranquil scene on the Llangollen Canal in Wales. Speed is limited to 4 knots on Britain's canal system so these traditional narrowboats require little power to push them along.

Displacement hull

These are traditional non-planing hull forms with a maximum speed that can be derived from the following formula:

Hull speed = 1.4 x $\sqrt{\text{waterline length}}$

Thus a hull with a waterline length of 25ft (7.6m) has an effective top speed of 7 knots.

These traditional types do not rise up like a planing boat. Instead they continue to push aside their own weight of water to form a bow and stern wave that increase in size as the speed goes up to the point where the boat is supported by the two waves and there is a big hollow in between. Once full hull speed is achieved, any further power applied will simply push the hull up its bow wave and leave the stern to sink down in the trough and create a great deal of wash and wasteful fuel consumption.

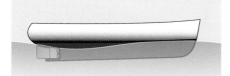

Displacement hull operating at its design speed

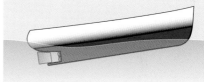

Hull pushed beyond its design speed

A Shetland 27 motor cruiser specifically designed for inland, estuary and coastal cruising, powering up the River Thames at nearly her designed displacement speed.

Semi-displacement hull

These are a hybrid of the two hull forms and combine the V-shape forward sections of the planing hull with a flat or rounded profile aft of the displacement hull. When pushed above displacement speed, this design type operates at the lower end planing mode speeds and provides a comfortable ride through heavy seas. Sometimes known as 'Nelson' hull types, these 'all weather' boats are popular as harbour-master launches and pilot boats and for recreational use in areas where strong swells are prevalent.

A Seaward 32 'Nelson' type motorboat cutting through the Solent chop. Below: A Nelson pilot boat used to meet ships entering port in any weather.

A Nelson 42 semi-displacement Police launch entering Yarmouth Harbour. These designs have the ability to cruise quietly or speed through heavy seas with equal ease.

Planing hull

These are designed to rise up on top of the water to reduce drag and wave-making resistance, then plane along the surface at high speed. The transition point between displacement and planing is known as 'hump speed'. This is when the boat suddenly accelerates forward just as if a turbo has kicked in when driving a car. Once a powerboat is planing, it requires less power to maintain this state, and throttles can be cut back to conserve fuel.

The sleek lines of a Riva 44 Rivarama planing at speed. Note how half the hull is riding clear of the water.

Deep V-planing hull

These are the most popular form of fast powerboat for fast offshore fishing and cruising. The sharp bow and V-shaped bottom, which carries all the way back to the transom, makes for a smoother ride over waves. Some designs have widely flared bows, which add buoyancy forward and limit any tendency for the hull to bury its nose when running down following seas. Spray rails, which deflect spray, also contribute to this 'lift'.

At slow speeds, the deep-V hull has more draft than a flat-planing hull. The deeper the V or angle of deadrise (often between 18° and 25°), the better the performance and ride will be in rough conditions. The trade-off is less speed than a flat planing hull in calmer conditions.

Spray rails

Chine

Angle of deadrise

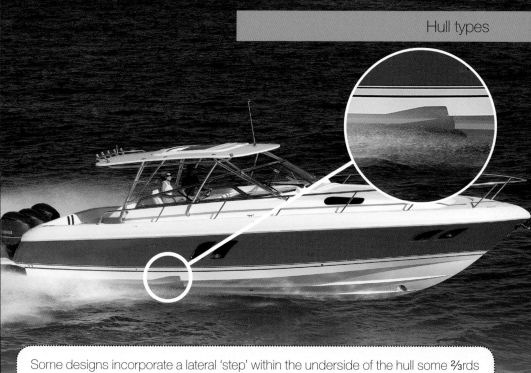

Some designs incorporate a lateral 'step' within the underside of the hull some ⅔rds of the way back from the bow to encourage air to vent under the aft hull sections. The bubbles of air that get sucked into the water flow act like ball bearings to reduce skin friction and increase speed or fuel economy (above).

Recently, Beneteau launched their own version of the stepped hull, called 'Air-Step'. This patented system pipes air through vents sited just below the gunwales on either side of the hull to an outlet on the centreline of the hull from where the flow fans out across the aft run. The effect of this air cushion is to improve both performance and handling of the boat.

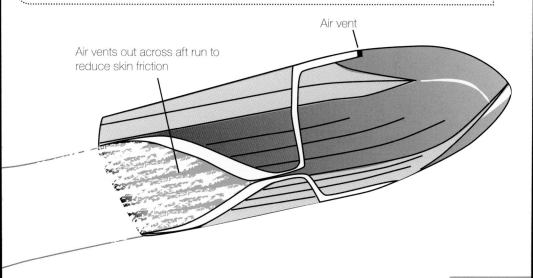

Air vent

Air vents out across aft run to reduce skin friction

Cathedral hull

The triple V-shaped planing monohull was another first for the American deep-V pioneer, Ray Hunt. His concept was first exploited by Boston Whaler in the USA and later developed by Dell Quay and Orkney Boats in England. The design offers a wide rectangular full-length cockpit, coupled with tremendous stability and load-carrying capabilities. The original designs gave a notoriously wet and bumpy ride when speeding into head seas, but this was overcome in later models which carry the centre V-shaped hull well forward of the two side pods and cut through the water much better.

These boats are popular as tenders, safety boats and harbour launches.

▶ Dell Quay Dory Sportsman

Length overall:	14ft	11in	(4.6m)
Beam:	6ft	5in	(2.0m)
Weight:			400kg
Engine options:			25–60hp
Builder: Fletcher Boats			
www.fletcher-boats.co.uk			

▶ Orkney Dory

Length overall:	14ft		(4.2m)
Beam:	5ft	11in	(1.8m)
Weight:			252kg
Engine options:			25–50hp
Builder: Orkney Boats Limited			
www.orkneyboatsltd.co.uk			

A Boston Whaler Outrage cathedral hull has been favoured by many harbourmasters as well as the US Coast Guard as a harbour patrol boat.

▶ Multihulls

Powered multihulls were first popularised in Australia and America where they are used as fast fishing boats. These twin-hulled designs marry the good stability characteristics of the cathedral hull with the sea keeping qualities of a deep-V. They also have the benefit of having a wide aft cockpit which makes an ideal fishing platform, and in larger versions like Glacier Bay Ocean Runner shown here, carry good accommodation in their twin hulls.

These boats are quite capable of cruising the open oceans, having crossed the Pacific, made the run across the Gulf Stream to Bermuda, and cruised the entire lengths of the east and west seaboards of America.

▶ Cat fishing boats

Powered catamarans are very popular as sports fishing boats and workboats. Not only are they fast and stable, but those built in alloy like this Allycat design from Australia, are strong and utilitarian. They are also light enough to launch and recover on a trailer tow behind a family car.

▼ Wave piercing hulls

For many years, Australian and New Zealand designers have led the world in wave piercing hull technology. These powered multihulls are characterised by their long, slender sharp-ended outer hulls with very little buoyancy at their bow, designed to 'pierce' through the waves rather than ride over them. Incat, the Tasmanian shipbuilder, has developed a series of high-speed car ferries, one of which holds the Hales Trophy for the fastest crossing of the Atlantic by a commercial ship.

In New Zealand, Craig Loomes who designed the 2008 round the world record breaker *Earthrace*, has developed a series of luxurious sports fishing boats from 40–70ft (12–21m) that use the same concept to very good effect. These wide-bodied craft not only offer enormous accommodation for their overall length, but can sprint along at 30 knots+, cruise comfortably into head and following seas at 25 knots, and impressively, have a range of 3,000 miles when making 10–15 knots.

Construction

Classic wooden boats

Wooden motorboats have more character but require more work than composite boats. If you don't enjoy maintenance as much as driving them, steer clear of these.

If you are bent on buying a classic, then a survey is essential. Rot is the most prevalent enemy and will manifest itself anywhere where rainwater gets trapped and soaks into the wood.

Vessels moored in salt water fare much better than those kept on a lake or river. Marinas, even those opening on to the sea, are often fed by fresh water streams, which results in a brackish water environment that is no kinder to wood than fresh water.

Wooden boats require regular maintenance to keep on top of a deteriorating atmosphere. Wood should never be allowed to go bare and requires annual painting.

A classic slipper stern launch beautifully restored by Peter Freebody & Co, based on the River Thames at Hurley.

Ideally, wooden boats should be stored under cover during the winter months in order to dry out ready for repainting in the spring, and this needs to be budgeted for when calculating annual costs.

Having said that, there are a large number of classic wooden boats from sleek slipper stern river launches to Riva and Chris*Craft open speedboats to be found in the brokerage columns, together with hot moulded fast offshore cruisers like the Fairey Marine Huntress, Huntsman and Swordsman built during the 1960s and '70s that are still going strong and maintaining their value.

A Riva Aquarama from the 1970s favoured by royalty and Holywood film stars. Each boat was crafted from a single mahogany tree to ensure matching grain throughout.

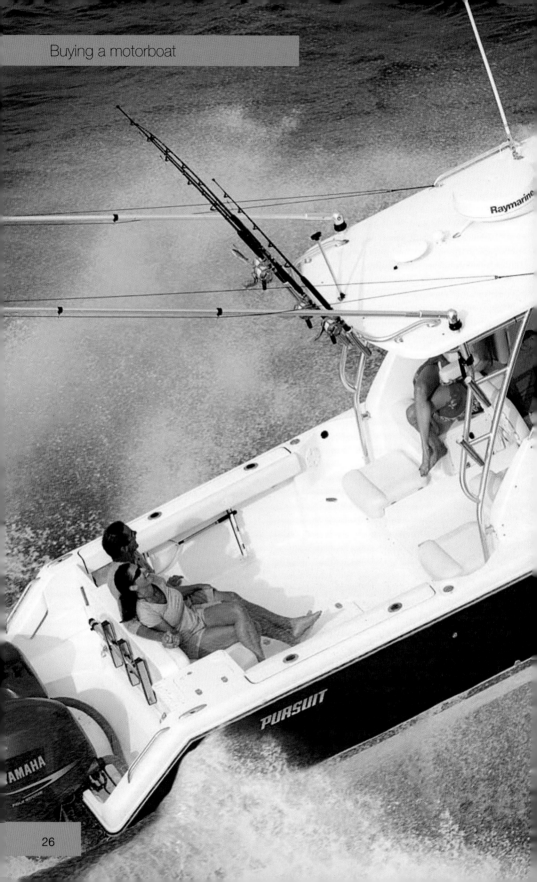

Glass fibre boats

Fibre-reinforced plastic boats are by far the most popular, being lighter and relatively low maintenance. They are long lasting and hold their value well. Indeed many of the early GRP motorboats moulded in the 1960s are still going strong and command good prices in the brokerage columns. Later models are often moulded using more exotic materials to the simple chopped strand fibreglass mat, and laminates can now incorporate Kevlar and even carbon fibre to provide greater strength without increasing overall weight.

When buying second-hand, look for any signs of stress cracks on corners, and star crazing within the gel coat around the hull and deck could signal clues to minor impact damage.

Check also for signs of osmosis. This water penetration through the outer gel coat manifests itself as small blisters below the waterline. This can be expensive to repair, requiring the gel coat to be planed off, the hull dried, and the affected areas re-coated with an epoxy based resin.

Automated moulding systems

Shelling boats out of a mould like peas from a pod has long been a boatbuilding utopia. But the road towards complete automation has been a hard one, not least because the initial set-up costs are infinitely more expensive than manual moulding. The 2008 recession led to a significant shake-up within the automated moulding industry, not because of any shortcomings in the construction methods but the fact that demand did not keep up with production.

Prior to mid-2009, many brand-names like Glastron, Four Winns and Larson were moulded using the VEC process which proved very successful and trouble free. The VEC computer controlled closed mould manufacturing process (below) continues and is now used to produce Larson, FinCraft and Seaswirl fibreglass boats with lifetime guarantees.

The VEC computer controlled closed mould manufacturing process.

Another successful automated production system is the Roto-mould process perfected by Triumph Boats in the US. These durable sports fishing boats (above) are produced like windsurfing boards, by charging powdered Roplene into an enclosed steel mould which is then heated to 260°C, and rotated. As the heat from the oven penetrates the mould, the powdered plastic starts to melt and stick to the interior surfaces. The process continues until layer after layer of material is built up and fused into a single, seamless piece that includes deck, gunwales, hull, storage boxes and transom. The result is a range of boats with remarkable strength, resilience and shock-absorbing characteristics. If you see them at a boat show, don't be surprised if the salesman hands you a sledgehammer to test this for yourself!

Aluminium or steel

Metal fabricated hulls are strong but require regular painting to minimise corrosion. Those with cabins can also suffer from condensation in winter months unless they are well insulated.

Steel is the most popular material for building canal narrowboats. Being flat bottomed with a standard width throughout their length, and simple pointed bow and rounded stern, these craft are easy to fabricate and maintain. They are also extremely tough and pretty well impervious to being banged against lock walls and other boats. For the same reason, steel is just as popular for building boats to cruise the European inland waterways.

Aluminium is lighter than steel but more costly. Bare alloy presents far less of a problem corrosion-wise because, unlike steel, the surface oxidises to form a natural protective coating. Aluminium is however very susceptible to electrolytic corrosion, especially in salt water which acts like battery acid, conducting electricity between dissimilar metals such as a bronze propeller, stainless steel prop shaft and the metal hull. Electrolytic action can even occur between two boats moored alongside each other, so it is imperative to have zinc anodes fitted to the hull. These act as sacrificial plates and are bolted to the hull close to the props and stern gear. Any electrolytic action then 'eats' the zinc before attacking the props, and need to be checked regularly and replaced before they dissolve completely.

Being light and hard wearing, aluminium is often used to fabricate tenders, workboats and fishing vessels. The material is also used to construct the superstructure above deck on steel hulls in order to reduce weight and lower the centre of gravity.

A typical aluminium 'bass' boat. Used as fishing and workboats, they are hardwearing and light enough to tow behind a car.

Steel is the perfect construction material for fabricating heavy displacement, slow-moving canal and river boats, helping them withstand to the knocks and scrapes they receive navigating locks and narrow waterways.

3 Propulsion systems

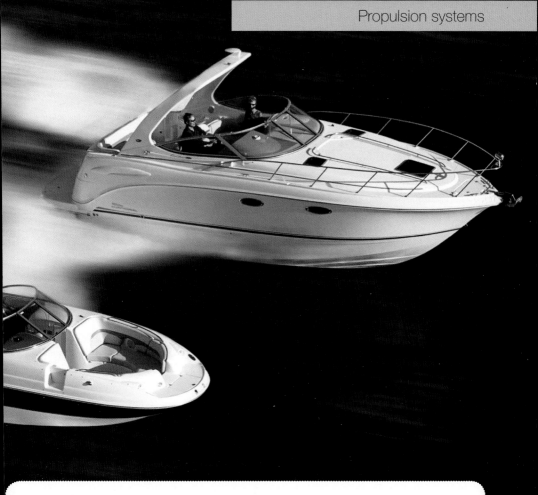

There are four types of propulsion – the outboard, the inboard, the inboard/outdrive and the waterjet. All rely on the screw propeller to provide the thrust.

In practice, propellers perform well below their theoretical pitch figures so it is vital that their diameter and pitch are matched to the size and expected performance of the boat. Most engine manufacturers have a computer programme to calculate the optimum prop size for a particular hull type and offer options to provide top-end speed, or increase load carrying performance.

Stainless steel propellers are strongest, but bronze is often the most cost effective material for thru-hull shaft driven boats. Aluminium props are common on outboards. Composite and plastic propellers are generally used for emergency situations.

When buying second-hand, check the propellers for nicks, rolled tips, or bent blades for any deformities will have an adverse effect on performance and can lead to engine damage caused through over-revving.

Outboards

The outboard motor has been around since 1909 and are now the most common form of propulsion within the marine leisure world, providing compact, weather proofed units from 1.5–300hp.

At one end of the market are the light, simple battery-powered electric auxiliaries used to power small tenders and provide super-quiet manoeuvrability when fishing. At the other are the sophisticated 2 and 3 litre models with electronic engine management systems providing race-bred performance. In between, is an enormous choice of engines, including 2 and 4-stroke, prop or jet power that carry well known names like Evinrude, Johnson, Honda, Mariner, Mercury, Suzuki and Yamaha.

The lighter 2-stroke engines have largely been phased out by the more complex 4-stroke models which offer greater fuel economy, quieter running with less exhaust emission, but 2-strokes are still available on the second-hand market.

TIP

The typical lifespan of an outboard run in salt water is 11–12 years. If you are looking to buy a second-hand boat, disregard the value of the engine if it is showing its age.

A lightweight battery powered outboard motor is ideal to power a small tender, and as an auxiliary to provide silent running when fishing.

Some manufacturers produce waterjet powered variants of the outboard which have the additional safety factor of an enclosed propeller.

Large outboards, now produce 350+ hp and are highly sophisticated.

Inboards

Most marine inboard engines are adapted car or truck motors, though some like Volvo Penta, Mercruiser and Yanmar are purpose made for the marine environment.

Inboard installations offer the ability to place the engine weight to greatest advantage, and are connected to the prop shaft either via a reduction gearbox or a V-drive. The greater the incline of the shaft, the less efficient the forward thrust. The exposed shafts, struts, P-brackets and rudders all contribute to parasitic drag, and quite apart from the vibration that shafts produce, they also lose a surprising amount of power from the friction generated by their rotation in the water.

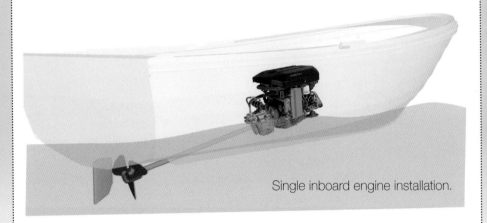

Single inboard engine installation.

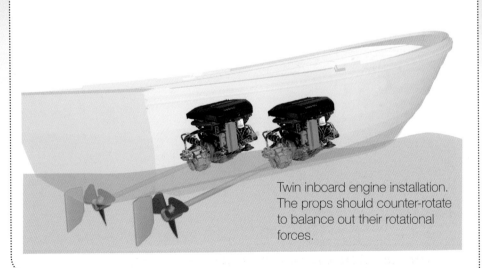

Twin inboard engine installation. The props should counter-rotate to balance out their rotational forces.

A Fairline 50 Flybridge twin screw motor cruiser, planing at 25 knots.

Inboard/Outdrives

The drag problems associated with standard inboard installations are largely overcome by the hybrid inboard/outdrive where an inboard engine drives a steerable outdrive leg. These have the advantage of a simple installation, lower noise and vibration levels, and the ability to raise and lower the leg like an outboard when navigating in shallow waters. They also allow the boat to take to the ground on a falling tide.

Their main disadvantage is that engine weight is centred well aft, which can cause boats, not designed specifically for these installations to bounce badly when heading into rough seas. Volvo's IPS forward facing drive system overcomes this by fitting the outdrive leg through the bottom of the hull which has the effect of moving the engine weight forward.

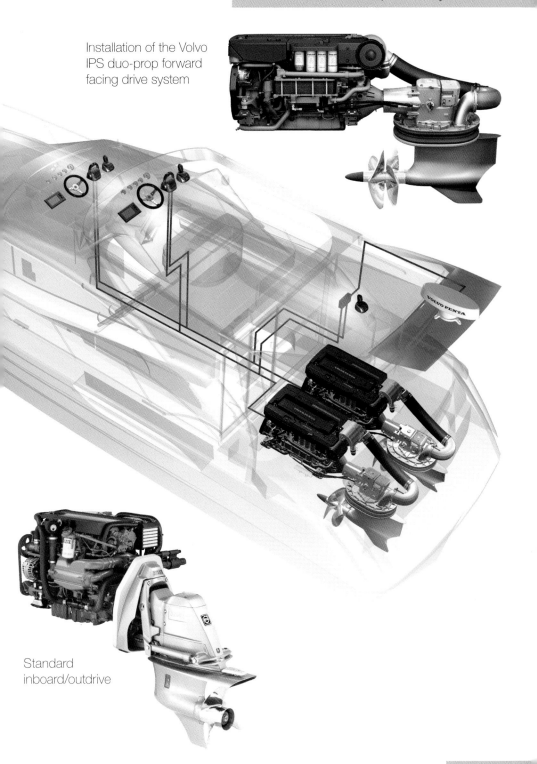

Installation of the Volvo
IPS duo-prop forward
facing drive system

Standard
inboard/outdrive

Waterjets

Waterjets like the Hamilton Jet and Castoldi range, generate thrust by forcing water in the opposite direction. Newton's Third Law of Motion stipulates that 'every action has an equal and opposite reaction', and waterjets work in the same way. That backward thrust is felt when holding a powerful fire hose.

The one-piece jet unit is mounted inboard at the back end of the boat with the nozzle cut through the transom and the water intake fits flush with the bottom of the hull. Water flow is accelerated through the narrowing diameter of the unit by an impeller, and discharged at high velocity through the nozzle. Steerage is achieved with twin rudders positioned either side of the nozzle to deflect the stream. Reverse is gained by lowering a deflector or 'bucket' over the stream to direct it back under the boat.

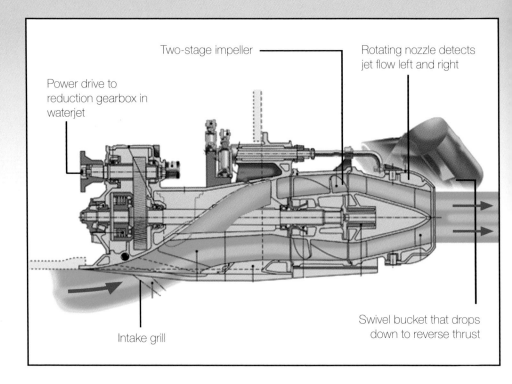

Two-stage impeller

Rotating nozzle detects
jet flow left and right

Power drive to
reduction gearbox in
waterjet

Swivel bucket that drops
down to reverse thrust

Intake grill

Cutaway of a Castoldi waterjet unit (above) and (right) a twin waterjet installation.

The waterjet is infinitely more controllable than any other propulsion system. By using the bucket to deflect the water downwards, the boat can be held in a stationary position, and in an emergency, reverse thrust will stop the boat, often within its own length. With no exposed moving parts, the units also offer complete safety to swimmers and wildlife, draft is minimised, and boats can operate in little more than their own depth of water.

Their one disadvantage is that weed, plastic bags and other flotsam can severely restrict the intake. The units are fitted with weed deflectors, but to clear them invariably entails stopping the engine. Jet units are not recommended in areas where there are high levels of weed or rubbish floating on the surface.

Bow and stern thrusters provide complete control

Bow/stern thrusters

Handling motor boats in tight situations and 'parallel parking' them has been made all the easier with the development of bow and stern thruster systems. These have an impeller running inside a transverse tube cut through the bow section or fastened to the transom to push the boat laterally to port or starboard. They are usually operated with a joystick from the steering position.

Impeller set in tube within the bow

Surface-piercing propeller drives

Racing, they say, improves the breed, and surface-piercing propeller drives, like trim tabs, have come straight off the back of high-performance race boats and are now being fitted to fast production models. They are designed to minimise propeller shaft inclination and reduce mechanical friction and cavitation. Traditional propellers produce considerable cavitation when under load, air bubbles that surface-piercing props ventilate on the surface, making them move water more efficiently and faster.

Another plus is that while inboard/outdrives lose 15–17% of their power through their complex gear drive, these losses are cut to 1–2% with the surface-piercing drives. They are also much lighter, offering a 75% weight saving over the outdrive and can handle much greater power. There is also no limit to the size of the propeller they can carry, allowing for a lighter-loaded, more efficient design.

Steering is achieved either with a rudder set immediately behind the propeller, or in the case of the Arneson Drive, by moving the entire propeller shaft (which rotates on a ball joint) from left to right, using an hydraulic ram attached to the outer end of the shaft.

Their disadvantage is a poor performance in reverse caused partially by the cleaver style propellers with their thick trailing edges, and the fact that the water flow is directed back onto to the transom. One solution is to fix baffle plates between the transom and propeller, which swing down to deflect the flow under the transom whenever reverse gear is selected.

Another problem comes at low speed when the surface propeller is running fully submerged and the top half is running in turbulence from the transom. The system then requires more torque to drive the propeller at a given rpm. This can be overcome by either directing the engine exhaust gasses into the water just ahead of the propeller or to install a 2-speed gearbox within the drive system to deliver the required torque.

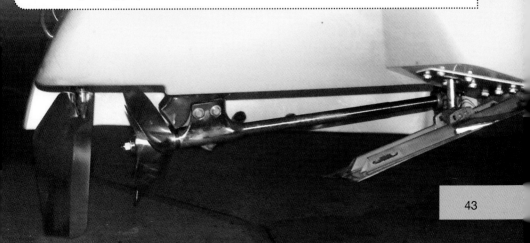

Surface-piercing propeller drive installation on a Sunseeker XS sports powerboat.

4
Motorboat types

▶ What type will best suit your needs?

The following pages profile a selection of powerboats that typify the wide selection available, including fishing boats, river and canal cruisers, centre console, deckboats, walk-around cuddy boats, bow riders, ski boats, sports and flybridge cruisers.

This is where heads rather than hearts should rule. Think first about the practical considerations. If you are planning to explore the inland waterways, there is no need for a high powered boat. If fishing is your bag, then a utilitarian boat may be far more practical
than one with a lavish interior.

A crew of four can enjoy a day out in a 17–19ft (5–6m) boat, but six would find this very cramped and will need something up to 21ft (6.4m). Six to eight people will need a 23–25ft boat, and nine or more will be crowded out in anything less than a 26ft boat. The manufacturer's plate will stipulate the maximum carrying capacity of individual designs (see page 84).

If young children are to be aboard, then their safety will be paramount. A deep cockpit makes for a safe playpen. Secure seating, a cabin or cuddy, and toilet facilities are other considerations to note.

▶ Trailer boats

Trailer boats can be an attractive proposition. They not only provide you with the versatility to explore different areas, but can be stored and maintained on their trailer at home, saving the considerable cost of a marina berth or mooring.

Towing regulations in many countries stipulate that the dry weight of the towing vehicle must, at a minimum, equal the weight of the loaden trailer, which must also be fitted with brakes. Within the EU, brakes are not required on fully laded trailers below 750kg and where the weight of the vehicle is at least twice the weight of the tow. From October 2012, all trailers used within the EU must have side as well as tail lights, requiring the car to be wired up with a 13-pin plug rather than the old 7-pin system. Some countries also restrict the driving age to those over 21 and you may be required to pass an additional driving test.

TIP

Before buying a boat, check that your vehicle meets the legal restrictions to tow the boat and its trailer. The car handbook will list the maximum safe towing weight.

▶ Second-hand boats

Pre-owned motorboats offer a very cost effective entry into boating. Most are moulded from glass reinforced plastic (GRP) and these have been a popular choice since the first of this kind were manufactured in the late 1960s and early '70s. It is quite possible to buy a small serviceable second-hand boat complete with engine and trailer for less than £2,000. Weekenders that double as ski boats can be found in the brokerage columns for under £10,000.

Compared to the latest offerings, these early examples are quite basic in appearance, especially in the cabin, so it is a question of finding an example that has benefitted from some tender loving care from a previous owner. Boats, especially those from well respected builders, hold their value remarkably well and you can expect to recover your initial investment, just as previous owners have done.

Early GRP moulded hulls were often reinforced with wood especially in the transom and longitudinal stringers. Beware of rot caused by water creeping in through the laminate.

An early Dawncraft 22 inland power cruiser, still going strong, navigating through the Stenson wide lock on the Trent and Mersey Canal at Derby.

You can check for this by walking around the cockpit and deck checking for any soft spots, and pulling on the engine or outdrive to see if there is any movement within the transom. These are expensive repairs and the best advice is to walk away from the deal.

Engines and their drives however, are the most expensive parts of a motorboat to replace, so if you are not mechanically minded yourself, call in an expert to give an opinion on their life expectancy.

Wooden motorboats like the Fairey Swordsman (below) built in 1966, remain very popular, and indeed have a classic value. The hulls were produced by laying up veneers of wood over a male mould then heat-curing the entire boat in a large oven. This technology, developed during the 2nd World War to build Mosquito fighter/bombers, has stood the test of time very well, though it is imperative to engage a surveyor to check for any signs of rot within the hull and deck structure before agreeing to purchase. Wooden boats require a lot more maintenance than GRP ones, so this too has to be a consideration.

These classic Fairey Swordsman sports powerboats, first built in 1966, are just as sought-after today and hold their values well, though being of wooden construction, require a survey before purchase.

▶ Ski boat

Fletcher Wakesport 17GTS Arrowstreak

Length overall:	17ft	1in	(5.1m)
Beam:		6ft 9in	(2.1m)
Weight:			960kg
Engine options:			1.7–4.3ltr inboard/ outdrive

Builder: Fletcher Boats

www.fletcher-boats.co.uk

The Fletcher Wakesport 17GTS Arrowstreak is a typical example of the specialist ski boats available, and is the smaller of two within the Fletcher range designed specifically for wakeboarding. They are similar in concept to the flat bottomed waterski tow boat with the same overhead towbar, but have a V-hull which produces a larger wake for the wakeboarder to jump over.

▶ Rigid bottom inflatable

Ribeye S Series 650

Length overall:	21ft	7in	(6.6m)
Beam:	8ft	3in	(2.5m)
Weight:			800kg
Max power::			150hp
Builder: Ribeye Ltd			
www.ribeye.co.uk			

The rigid bottom inflatable (RIB) was first developed by Atlantic College in Wales for Avon as an all weather inflatable. This resulted in the Atlantic 21 which the RNLI adopted as a fast inshore lifeboat. Avon continue to produce their Searider series and the concept has been developed by a number of manufacturers including AB Marine, Cirrus, Europa, Humber, Novurani, Pirana, Ribcraft, Ribeye, Scorpion, Tornado, Valiant, Williams and Zodiac.

▶ Fishing boat

Orkney Vanguard 190

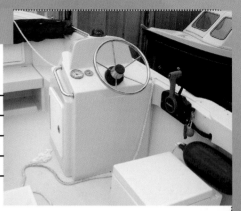

Length overall:	19ft 4in	(5.9m)
Beam:	7ft 5in	(2.3m)
Weight:		750kg
Max. power:		100hp
Builder: Orkney Boats Limited		

www.orkneyboatsltd.co.uk

Orkney, one of Britain's largest small boat manufacturers has been producing traditional simulated clinker grp fishing boats for more than four decades. The latest in their range are the TT designed Vanguard 170 and 190 outboard powered open fishing boats (below), but many examples of their original Orkney 16 and 19ft Longliner models are still going strong and commanding good prices within the brokerage columns.

▶ Fishing boat

Merry Fisher 725

Length overall:	23ft	5in	(7.2m)
Waterline length:	22ft	9in	(7.0m)
Beam:	9ft	2in	(2.8m)
Draft:	1ft	11in	(0.6m)
Weight:			1850kg
Max. power:			150hp
Builder: Jeanneau			

www.jeanneau.com

The Merry Fisher range of sports fishing boats manufactured by French builder Jeanneau, is one within a wide selection of deckhouse sports fishing boats that can be trailed behind a large car and perform well in open waters. Other manufactures include Beneateau, Hardy, Orkney Boats, and Trusty Motor Boats.

▶ Centre console

245 Centre Console

Length overall:	24ft 6in	(7.4m)
Beam:	8ft 6in	(2.6m)
Draft:	1ft 9in	(0.53m)
Weight:		1543kg
Max. power:		350hp
Builder: EdgeWater Power Boats		

www.ewboats.com

Fast, deep-V centre console sports fishing boats have long been popular in America because of their roomy layout and go-anywhere appeal. Manufacturers include Boston Whaler, Edgewater, Persuit, Pro-Line and Regulator Marine. These boats come equipped with bait boxes, fish holds, rod holders and even ice boxes to keep the beers cool. Larger models including the EdgeWater 245, have an enclosed toilet compartment built into the console.

▶ Bow rider

Chaparral 180 SSi

Length overall:	18ft 3in	(5.6m)
Beam:	7ft 2in	(2.2m)
Draft:	1ft 9in	(0.5m)
Weight:		953kg
Engine options:	225hp inboard/ outdrive	

Builder: Chaparral Boats

www.chaparralboats.com

Bow rider – speedboats with a seating area in the bow, forward of the windshield are another popular export from America where manufacturers like Chaparral, Glastron and Seafox produce them in large numbers.

These trailerable boats are invariably equipped with a swim platform, sunbed over the engine compartment. They are powerful enough to double as a ski boat.

▶ Walk around

Beneteau Flyer 850 Sun Deck

Length overall:	27ft	1in	(8.3m)
Waterline length:	26ft	3in	(8m)
Beam:	9ft	8in	(2.9m)
Draft:	2ft	6in	(0.8m)
Weight:			2730kg
Max. power:			400hp (twin engine)

Builder: Beneteau SA

www.beneteau.com

'Walk around' is an American term for trailerable weekenders with a live-aboard forward cabin, toilet compartment and foredeck with safety rails around it. Manufacturers include Beneteau, Boston Whaler, Edgewater, Fletcher, Glastron Persuit, Robelo and Seafox.

▶ Canal/narrow boat

Length overall:		40–70ft
		(12.2–21.3m)
Beam:	6ft 10in	(2.1m)
Draft:	2ft	(0.6m)
Engine options:		Diesel or steam
Builder: Canal Boatbuilders Association		
www.c-b-a.co.uk		

Narrow boats are unique to the British canals, though these distinct cruisers can also be found on European waterways. The design is based on the original working barges from the 18th century and many are highly decorated to recall that era. The maximum beam is set at 6ft 10in (2.08m) and are invariably built at 10ft increments from 40–70ft overall, in order to fit in the locks. These boats are usually built to order by local craftsmen sited on canal sides right around Britain. A list of builders is available from www.c-b-a.co.uk

▶ River cruiser

Shetland 27i

Length overall:	26ft	6in	(8.1m)
Beam:	9ft	6in	(2.9m)
Draft:	2ft	2in	(0.6m)
Displacement:			3 tons
Max. power:			110hp

Builder: Shetland Boats

www.shetlandboats.co.uk

Europe's inland waterways play host to a wide variety of distinctive cruising boats, from the heavy steel Dutch motor cruisers, the wide beamed boats unique to the Norfolk Broads with their fold-down screens and sliding coachroofs and fold-down screens, to the inland and estuary motorboats built by the likes of Alpha Craft, Aquafibre, Shetland Boats and Viking Seamaster. All are flat bottomed or with a shallow V-hull to provide maximum stability, and have interiors designed to maximise living space and provide value for money.

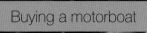

▶ Sports cruiser

Fairline Targa 40

Length overall:	41ft 10in	(12.53m)
Beam:	12ft 1in	(3.68m)
Draft:	3ft	(0.9m)
Displacement:		8.7 tons
Max. power:		700hp
		(twin engine)

Builder: Fairline Boats Ltd

www.fairline.com

Open deck offshore sports cruisers are designed to soak up the Mediterranean sun and provide sumptuous living below decks. They are available in various lengths from 38–80ft (11.6–24.4m) and offer exhilarating performance. Manufacturers include Bavaria, Beneteau, Chris*Craft, Fairline, Jeanneau, Magnum, Princess, Riva, Sealine, and Sunseeker. One thing they all have in common are interiors designed to impress, with queen-sized beds, lounge areas with galley and separate bathroom, laid out to provide comfort during a fast run from Cannes to Corsica and overnight stay.

▶ Flybridge cruiser

Sealine F42

Length overall:	44ft	7in	(13.6m)
Beam:	14ft	8in	(4.48m)
Draft:	3ft	10in	(1.15m)
Weight:			12,900kg

Builder: Sealine International Limited

www.sealine.com

Flybridge cruisers are more popular in northern climes where they provide a more sheltered ride than the sports cruiser when the weather is unsettled. If conditions turn bad, then dual controls mirror the flybridge in the safe dry confines of the bridge saloon, one deck below.

Manufacturers include Bavaria, Bertram, Beneteau, Fairline, Jeanneau, Ferretti, Princess, Riva, Sealine, Storebro, and Sunseeker. The flybridge often doubles as an al fresco wet bar and barbecue area, with large saloons that open onto sheltered stern cockpits. Below decks can be a revelation in sumptuous living, with designers packing a remarkable number of ensuite cabins into the limited space between the bow and engine room.

▶ **Trawler yachts**

Grand Banks Heritage 41 EU

Length overall:	46ft	2in	(14.1m)
Waterline length:	37ft	11in	(11.6m)
Beam:	15ft	8in	(4.8m)
Draft:	3ft	9in	(1.1m)
Weight:			18,235kg
Builder: Grand Banks			
www.grandbanks.com			

This Heritage 41 EU is a hybrid semi-displacement motor yacht that combines the excellent sea-keeping abilities of a deep-sea trawler with the ability to cruise at 20 knots. They are increasingly popular. Builders include Beneteau, Cheoy Lee, Grand Banks and Trader Yachts. All have a flybridge and pilot house, plenty of accommodation below decks and the facilities and range to explore remote areas of the world. Most manufacturers build to order, and allow for a good deal of customisation with the interior design.

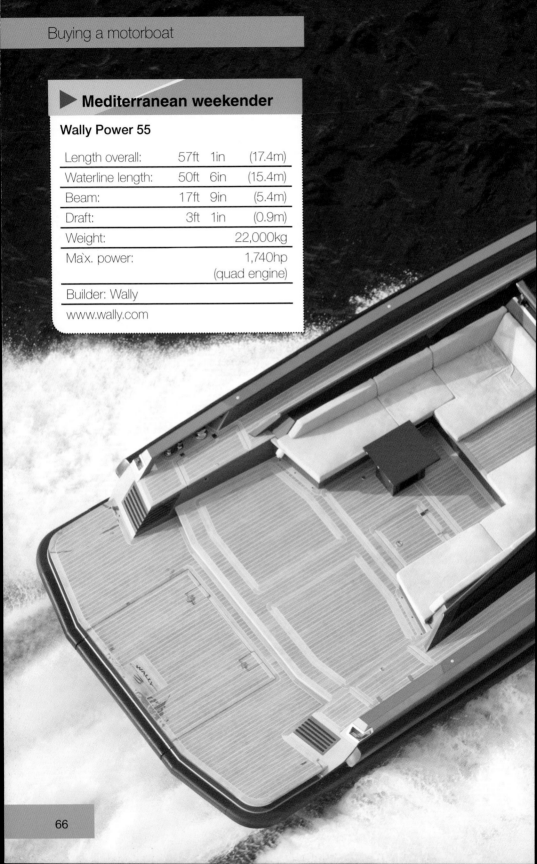

▶ Mediterranean weekender

Wally Power 55

Length overall:	57ft	1in	(17.4m)
Waterline length:	50ft	6in	(15.4m)
Beam:	17ft	9in	(5.4m)
Draft:	3ft	1in	(0.9m)
Weight:			22,000kg
Max. power:			1,740hp
			(quad engine)

Builder: Wally

www.wally.com

Beautiful, ostentatious and overtly sporty, these Mediterranean motorboats built by Wally, Riva and Chris*Craft are the ultimate speed boats designed to rush from point to point, make an impression and provide 5-star living below decks when the sun goes down. The Wally 55 is powered by four large Volvo Penta engines giving her a speed of 40 knots. If you have to ask the price, you probably can't afford one!

To buy, share or charter?

We take great pride in owning our own boat, but is it cost-effective? If usage is going to be limited, divide the annual cost by the number of times you are likely to use her. If the answer proves to be prohibitive, here are some alternatives.

▶ Shared ownership

Boats are best maintained when they are used regularly. If you visualise using your boat during one or two weeks or weekends a month during the season, it may make sense to share ownership with one or more friends or members of the family. This way, the boat will not only remain in good order, but individual running costs are reduced proportionately too, giving the group the option of buying a bigger or better boat, or can afford to have the work done professionally.

By sharing costs and usage two or three ways, no one becomes a slave to the boat. Knowing that you have use of it one week in three allows you to slot in other interests and perhaps cruise a wider area with one group taking over the boat from other at pre-arranged venues so that you never get bored using the same stretch of water all the time.

But what happens if there is a family or friendship split? Even the best of friends can fall out, so it makes sense to either draw up a simple contract or letter of understanding, setting out exactly what must happen if one party wants to sell their share. This is essential if the boat is subject to a joint loan or mortgage. The most equitable way is to call in a marine surveyor to give a market value of the boat. Then the other parties either buy them out or the boat is sold and the proceeds split after all outstanding costs have been met.

TIP

Agreement
Shared ownership has a lot of advantages for those expecting to get only limited use, but pick your partners carefully. You need to agree exactly what is expected from each shareholder in terms of maintenance and cost sharing, as well as usage.

TIP

Try before you buy

Some manufacturers can arrange for you to charter one of their boats to try out for size before you buy. They may even discount the charter if you go ahead with the deal.

▶ Time-share

Boat partnership programmes operated by big charter companies like The Moorings provide the opportunity to purchase a new 37 or 47ft cruising power cat at a discount, and include her in their charter fleet. You then have use of her, or any other of their boats, power or sail, for up to 12 weeks each year. This allows you to choose a different cruising area each time, taking in popular cruising grounds around the Great Barrier Reef, Belize, the Caribbean, Mexico, Phuket or the Seychelles. At the end of the 5-year contract, the boat is sold and you get most of your investment back.

Through The Moorings power yacht ownership scheme, owners pay the full purchase price of the yacht and place it into the charter fleet. You then receive a fixed monthly income that more than covers the loan repayments, and face no further expense. At the end of the contract, the owner is free to take over any further payments owed on the boat, sell her, or trade-in towards the purchase of a new vessel.

▶ Charter

This cuts out all concerns about tying up your capital, and being restricted to set periods for using your boat. You can charter for a weekend, week or three and everything can be taken care of, including the victualling. You then have the choice of chartering a bare boat or having a skipper onboard to take charge of navigation and berthing at ports of call.

6
What can I afford?

There is much more to the cost of owning than the price tag or mortgage. To get a complete picture of how big that hole in the water will be, use this work sheet to bring other costs in focus.

▼ Item	Annual cost
1. **Monthly repayments x 12**	
2. **Registration & harbour fees**	
3. **Insurance**	
4. **Mooring fees**	
5. **Fuel & oil**	
6. **Maintenance/repairs, including lift outs**	
7. **Winter storage**	
▶ **Total**	

▶ New vs second-hand

Most boats have an extraordinarily long life. Many of the first glassfibre moulded designs produced from the mid-1960s and onwards are still going strong and commanding good prices. If you want to buy new, that is fine, but the same amount of money could buy you a bigger second-hand motorboat. But remember, the running costs will be bigger too.

▶ New boats

▶ Payment

If you are buying new from stock, then the purchase should be just as straightforward as buying a car. You organise the finance, pay the invoice, and the boat is yours. It only gets complex when ordering a new boat to be built. This can take anything up to a year to complete and will involve a series of stage payments. It is essential to safeguard these payments against the possibility of the builder or their agent going bust.

Treat your boat purchase as if it were a property. Some motor yachts cost as much as a house anyway, so give serious consideration to having a lawyer represent your interests. There are just too many sorry tales of customers losing their money during the 2009–11 recession, not to act cautiously.

The builder or their agent will undoubtedly offer you a 'standard' contract of purchase. What safeguards does this provide?

▼ **The important points to note within a contract are:**

1. The price should be fixed and include any non-standard items

2. It should contain a full specification or inventory

3. Delivery: The date should be fixed – have a penalty clause inserted to compensate for loss of use if this is delayed

4. Completion should be subject to sea trials

5. Warranties: Insist on having the extent of warranties and 'free' after sales service specified

▼ Acceptance trials:

1. Does she float on her marks?

2. Does she perform to expectations?

3. Does she run level or have a tendency to ride on one chine – ie at an angle?

4. Are the gauges accurate and electronics working, including the bilge pumps? Check all electronics and moving parts

5. Does the inventory match the contracted specification?

▶ Safeguarding stage payments

Money held by a solicitor in a 'client account' is ring-fenced by the terms and conditions of the licence they operate under, but too often, a 'client account' is all too easy to dip into when cash flow runs short. Letters of credit are also only as watertight as the terms and conditions written into them.

Is the initial deposit returnable in the event of cancellation, or is it part of the payment plan? The simplest way to secure this is to spread the payments across a number of credit cards. Then, in the event of the agent or builder going out of business, you can make a claim against the card companies.

The purpose of stage payments is to fund the cost of equipment and materials during the construction process. One way to secure these payments is to stipulate within the contract exactly what those assets are: the mouldings, engine, spars, sails, electronics and furnishings etc. Then ensure that moulding and part numbers are listed as addenda to the contract. Under UK law, this then gives you clear title of ownership over the items listed.

Visit the yard as often as possible to photograph progress and ensure your name and hull number are indelibly marked on each item. This way you have proof of what you have title to. Then, should the company go into Receivership, you do at least own the unfinished hull and accessories, and the only headache is having it completed.

Elsewhere within the European Union and in many other parts of the world, however, this 'clear title of ownership' is far from clear. Then the only safe way to secure stage payments is to take out insurance against the loss. This will add 1–2% to the cost of the boat and, in some cases, the builder may be prepared to share half this cost. It is a good point for negotiation.

▶ Insurance

Check that the builder's insurance adequately covers the boat during construction (especially if you have title to the hull). If not, then you need to arrange your own insurance.

▶ Certification

All new boats must be built to comply with European Directives and be CE compliant, and come with EU technical data books. If a boat is to be used for charter it must comply with the relevant Code of Practice for commercial use. Ensure that these items are covered in the contract.

▶ Value added tax (VAT)

If you are a EU resident intending to use the boat in EU waters, then VAT must be paid. The same applies if you are importing the boat from outside the European Union. Ensure that the bill of sale lists the VAT element. You will need to show this whenever you voyage to another country and when you sell the boat.

▶ Small Ship Registration (SSR)

If finance is being obtained, most lenders will insist upon Part I registration of the boat in order for the loan company to register their interest. This also provides proof of ownership (as of date of registration) and will assist the process when selling. Large motorboats will have to have a tonnage survey, so this needs to be organised with the builder prior to hand-over so that registration can take effect on delivery.

Part II SSR is more informal and has no legal standing, but the certificate is sufficient to show proof of title when sailing abroad.

▶ Second-hand

First rule: Buy quality, not quantity. With boats that require a lot of restoration, don't under-estimate the cost. It is often cheaper to buy a new boat than buy new parts.

▶ Agreement

In many countries, a verbal agreement between two parties constitutes a binding contract, but without documentation, any problems that follow can be fraught with difficulties. A friend bought an amateur-built boat from the builder's widow after her husband had died, thinking that the quick cash deal would save him money and her a lot of anguish. Then came the problem of proving VAT had been paid. Undoubtedly it had been, but without paperwork there was no proof, and the purchaser had to pay it again, in order to resell the boat.

Then there is the second problem of proving ownership. Does the seller actually have title to the boat? One scam I came across in the world of classic boats is multiple selling. Two people thought that they had bought the boat and both had already paid a deposit on the laid up hull. It just happened that both also shared the same hairdresser, and being an inveterate gossip, he told the second 'purchaser' that a previous customer had just bought this 'classic'. That set alarm bells ringing, and sure enough the seller was trying to double his money and run. The second purchaser never did get his deposit back.

It is sensible to use one of the standard purchase forms available from national sailing authorities like the Royal Yachting Association (RYA). Where the cost of the vessel is substantial, then engage a marine lawyer to ensure that the transaction proceeds without a hitch.

Whether purchasing from the owner or a broker (who like an estate agent acts for the seller), consider the following:

▼ **The most important things to consider are:**

1. **The condition of the boat**

2. **Has VAT been paid?**

3. **Does the seller actually have the right to sell the boat?**

4. **Is the vessel subject to a mortgage?**

Unless you are buying a small value trailer boat and are satisfied by its visual condition, it is prudent to make any agreement 'subject to survey'. Then, even if a deposit has been paid, any problems picked up by the surveyor not disclosed by the seller, allows you to re-negotiate the price, or terminate the contract and demand your deposit back. It is also important to ensure that your surveyor has professional insurance just in case they miss something that materialises after the yacht has been bought. Don't rely on a survey provided by the seller.

Ensure that the seller produces evidence of VAT payment on the boat before parting with your deposit. The same applies to proof of ownership. If the yacht is registered, then this will name the ultimate owner, but also look for receipts that name the seller.

▼ Title documentation should include:

1. **Part 1 registration**

2. **Builder's certificate**

3. **Previous bills of sale**

4. **Evidence of Recreational Craft Directive (RCD) compliance**

5. **Evidence of VAT status (if within the EC)**

Check to see if the vessel is subject to a mortgage just as you would with the title documents for a property. If the boat is subject to a marine mortgage or a loan, this should be listed on the vessel's registration documents and recorded in the Small Ships' Register. Unfortunately, not all loans are recorded this way, and you may still get a visit from a finance company with the right to take the boat you have just bought, to recover the unpaid loan. A good contract may not prevent this occurring but it does give you the right of action against the seller. If there is a loan, ensure that this is discharged before completion.

▶ RCD compliance

The Recreational Craft Directive (RCD) is a piece of EU legislation that applies to all recreational craft between 8.2ft (2.5m) and 78.7ft (24m) brought into or offered for sale within the EU. Boats must comply with specific ISO standards, although equivalent standards can apply. Evidence of compliance can be found on the yacht's HIN/CIN (Hull/Craft identification number) on the builder's plaque. This is a 14-digit number containing the manufacturer's code, year of build and model year. There should also be a paper document, often found in the back of the owner's manual. The builder's invoice and/or certificate may also list the HIN. The CE mark should also be displayed on the plaque.

There are a few exemptions from the RCD. Boats that can show they were in the EU before 16th June 1998 when this legislation came into force, are exempt, as are boats

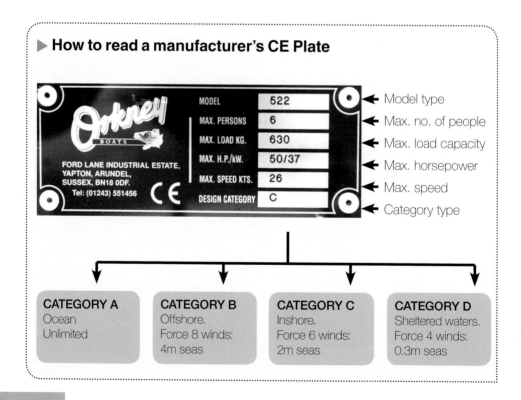

▶ How to read a manufacturer's CE Plate

MODEL	522	← Model type
MAX. PERSONS	6	← Max. no. of people
MAX. LOAD KG.	630	← Max. load capacity
MAX. H.P./kW.	50/37	← Max. horsepower
MAX. SPEED KTS.	26	← Max. speed
DESIGN CATEGORY	C	← Category type

FORD LANE INDUSTRIAL ESTATE, YAPTON, ARUNDEL, SUSSEX, BN18 0DF. Tel: (01243) 551456

CATEGORY A	CATEGORY B	CATEGORY C	CATEGORY D
Ocean	Offshore.	Inshore.	Sheltered waters.
Unlimited	Force 8 winds: 4m seas	Force 6 winds: 2m seas	Force 4 winds: 0.3m seas

that have been built solely for racing, gondolas and commercial vessels such as fishing and workboats. Vessels used for charter are not included in this category.

Part-finished boats and those built from scratch by a home builder are also exempt from RCD certification, provided the builder retains ownership of the vessel for at least five years from the date that the vessel was first put into commission. Professionally built hulls supplied for fit-out will have an Annex 3 Declaration, which is the builder's certification that the hull has been built in accordance with the RCD.

▶ Buying abroad

Boats being brought into use within the EU for the first time must comply with the RCD. On arrival, privately imported boats will be assessed for compliance. Some US boats are built to the RCD and have the required documentation, but check before you buy. If the engine does not meet EU requirements, for instance, this will need to be replaced, so it may not be economic to import the boat. Surveyors are best placed to give professional guidance. VAT will be payable on import.

Boats built in the EU since 1998 will have documentation that they complied with the RCD when first offered for sale, but vessels built within the EU prior to this date remain exempt unless they have been sold outside the EU and then re-imported. If any of the paperwork is missing then the authorities could well impound the boat the moment you try to move her.

The most common problems stem from outstanding claims for unpaid bills, and vessels that have overstayed their temporary import permit. One solution is to pay a local broker to check all this out. Another is to offer to pay for a crew to deliver the boat to another port and complete the deal there. Then it is up to the owner to ensure that the paperwork is up to scratch.

▶ Finance

The cheapest method is to pay for it out of savings, but then not too many of us have the luxury of a mega bank balance. What are the alternatives?

▶ Marine mortgage

A marine mortgage is registered in accordance with the UK Merchant Shipping Act 1993 and secured on the new or second-hand boat that it is financing, in a similar way that a house secures a property loan. Banks will normally lend up to 80% of the value of the boat over a period of 10 to 15 years. They also offer fixed or variable interest rate options and allow owners to make full or partial early repayments without penalty. Marine mortgages usually start at £100,000.

▶ Secured or unsecured bank loan

This is the simplest way to finance the purchase of a boat valued at less than £100,000. Rates will be cheaper if the amount can be secured against property or other investments. These are often limited to a 5 year term.

▶ Credit card

The quickest but most expensive way to pay, but OK if you plan to pay off the balance within the interest-free period. If you are not taking possession of the boat immediately, this is also the simplest way to insure against default or failure to deliver which will be covered by the card insurance policy.

▶ Other ways to raise finance

If you have substantial equity in a property, borrow against this. It is likely to be the cheapest form of finance.

▶ Treat the boat as a business asset

To do this, the boat must realise an income from charter, entertaining or as a training boat. You may be taxed for personal use of the boat as a benefit in kind.

▶ Sponsorship

If the boat has a high profile or is used for racing, you may be able to attract commercial sponsorship and receive payment for hospitality and branding on hull and sails.

▶ US tax breaks

In the US, you may be able to claim interest payments back when filing your federal income tax return, if the boat is equipped with a head and galley, because the asset can be treated for tax purposes as a second home. Don't forget to save your fuel receipts each time you top up the tanks. A portion of the excise tax on fuel is used by the Government to maintain roads, which some owners reclaim. Check the IRS website for latest details: www.irs.gov.

▶ Fuel consumption

Fuel is likely to be the single biggest running cost, and since leisure boaters throughout the EU now pay duty on red diesel, the weekend fuel bill has trebled. Fuel consumption then is a major consideration when deciding the type of boat you can afford to run.

Since red diesel is also used for heating, which is duty free, the authorities are currently allowing boat owners a 'no questions asked' 16% discount at the pump in recognition of the heating element within the price. This represents a 60/40 split of duty between propulsion and heating. Owners are entitled to claim a refund of all the duty at the pump, providing all the fuel oil is used for heating, and they may well be asked to prove this by revenue officers.

▼ Heating apart, where does the fuel go?

35%	simply goes up in smoke heating the atmosphere
25%	is given up in heat absorption in the surrounding water
10%	goes towards overcoming wave resistance
7%	to overcome skin friction
6%	goes towards wave formation and prop wash
2%	is wasted in friction at the propeller shaft
1%	goes towards overcoming air resistance

This leaves a pitiful 14% of the fuel you buy being used for its prime purpose of turning the propeller!

Fuel cost is one issue; capacity to carry it onboard is another. Smaller motorboats are often limited to carrying two 27 litre portable tanks, which can limit range considerably.

This outboard powered Seafox 200XT sports fishing boat shows the open space available within these centre console designs.

▶ Outboard engines

The latest direct injected 4-stroke engines such as the Johnson/Evinrude FICHT and Mercury OptiMax models are 40% more economical than even a well tuned 2-stroke engine, which explains why most outboard manufacturers have dropped these from their range. A 150hp 4-stroke outboard will burn approximately 68 litres of fuel per hour when at peak power – pretty much flat out. Fuel consumption decreases considerably at cruising speeds.

How much fuel you need to carry depends on the type of boat:

- A typical 30ft displacement hull powered by a 25hp diesel engine cruising at 75% of top speed, will consume approximately 10 litres an hour.
- A 40ft sports fishing boat powered by twin 370hp engines pushing her along at 40 knots by comparison, will consume 275 litres per hour in flat water. If conditions are rough, not only will you need to throttle back, but fuel consumption can easily double!
- As a rule of thumb, modern diesel engines consume 0.25 litres of fuel for every hp used and a petrol engine uses 0.45 litres.
- Petrol engines are at their most efficient when running at between 60–75% of full power.
- Diesel engines by comparison are at the optimum at around 80%.
- Planing hull forms use much more fuel than displacement boats, though consumption is cut considerably when throttles are pulled back once the boat is planing. Another economy consideration is whether the hull is clean or fouled. A freshly scrubbed boat will consume 25% less fuel than one that is weeded.

▼ How much will she cost to run?

Boat type	Litres per mile
6m RIB with single outboard at 30 knots	0.9
8m displacement river cruiser at 5 knots	1.5
15m twin screw semi-displacement boat at 15 knots	4.5
15m twin screw fast cruising hull	6.5
20m twin screw fast cruising hull	13

Surveys: the key elements

7

TIP

Ensure that the surveyor is qualified to survey the construction type of the vessel, and carries third party indemnity insurance.

If the boat of your choice is costing a substantial amount then, just like a house purchase, a professional should survey it. If you are buying her second-hand, and borrowing money to purchase her, then the lender may insist on it. The Insurance company may also want sight of the report before confirming the quotation.

▶ Key points about a survey

The surveyor should be qualified to inspect the construction type of your vessel. Not all are. Check if they are members of the International Institute of Marine Surveying (IIMS). This is an independent, non-political organisation that lists specialist surveyors and marine consultants in every corner of the globe. Their website, www.iims.org.uk, offers a search facility to locate a surveyor close to you who will abide to a clear code of practice.

A condition survey provides a professional opinion on the structural condition of visible aspects of the boat only, and the report should not be considered as a schedule of works, though it will certainly assist those preparing an estimate for repair or refurbishment. Hull condition is assessed using non-destructive methods of examination such as ultrasound and moisture meters, and the report is limited to the sample areas where the substrate paint is scraped away.

The surveyor will note whether the hull has undergone osmosis treatment, but not disturb the epoxy resin coating that has been applied. The readings from the ultrasound and damp meters, coupled with the practical test of tapping suspect areas of the hull, will give an indication to the surveyor whether further exploratory work is required to check for damp, delamination, and voids.

Likewise, the engine and machinery are given a visual inspection only, and the surveyor will limit his report to signs of corrosion, oil and water leaks. The content of tanks are not tested for contaminants unless you specifically ask for this to be done. Water and biological contamination in the fuel tank can be a particular problem.

Hull fastenings — stop-cocks and other thru-hull fittings etc. — are not drawn out for inspection unless you ask for this to be done. The same applies to the testing of doors, hatches and windows for water tightness.

The report will reflect the experience of the surveyor at looking at similar craft and construction methods. He will know instinctively where damp is likely to lie, where rot or corrosion could be prevalent and where problems are likely to arise in the future. His report will be thorough, have an action plan, and a valuation based not on its replacement cost, but the retail values achieved by vessels of a similar type and condition.

A professional surveyor will not only highlight any structural concerns, and provide a list of items that need attention, but his report will give you peace of mind that problems will not appear later.

If you decide against having a professional survey, here is a checklist to work through.

✓ Hull Checklist

☐ 1. Look at the transom and check the hull identification number. Does it match the number on the registration document?

☐ 2. GRP boats: Take a small rubber hammer or the handle end of a screwdriver, and tap the hull lightly at short intervals across the whole area of the hull. If there is a sudden change of note, this can indicate osmosis, voids or delamination.

☐ 3. Wooden boats: Check for black discolouration at joints and plank ends. This is a clear sign of the first stage of rot. Use a sharp bradawl to test suspect areas like the garboard strakes for softness – another sign of rot.

☐ 4. Steel hulls: Check for corrosion. How thin is the plating? An ultrasound test may be required.

☐ 5. Mismatched paint. This could indicate that the boat has been damaged in the past. If you were not informed of any repairs, what else have you not have been told about?

☐ 6. Does the propeller shaft turn true?

☐ 7. Take hold of the prop and check for shaft movement. If there is, this suggests a worn cutlass bearing.

☐ 8. Does the propeller have any nicks on the leading edges of the blades? These will lessen its performance.

☐ 9. Do any of the bronze fittings show signs of pinkness or pitting? This is a sign that the boat has suffered from electrolytic action between dissimilar metals (bronze and stainless steel for instance).

☐ 10. Check the sacrificial anodes close to the prop shaft and rudder for signs of pitting. Do they need to be replaced?

Damp meter readings at regular points around the hull provide the best indication of the porosity of the gel coat or paint system.

Non-invasive testing. The surveyor will scrape away small sections of paintwork at regular intervals around the hull to check for any breakdown in the gel coat. This boat had already undergone extensive osmosis treatment, but pin holes through the epoxy coating were still visible.

Bronze P-brackets and propellers can be badly affected by electrolysis, not just because of stainless steel prop shafts but the close proximity of steel bathing platforms and rudder assemblies. Often, the only way to check is to scrape away paintwork.

Check the zinc anodes. Do they need replacing? The sacrificial plates bolted on the outside of the hull will give a good indication as to whether the boat suffers from electrolysis.

The same applies to the rudder. If there is any sign of 'pinkness' within the bronze fittings – and this will be most prevalent on the tips of the propeller blades – then electrolytic action has occurred and the metal will be severely weakened and need to be replaced.

The deck takes a good deal of wear and tear and provides a good indication of the vessel's overall condition.

☑ Deck Checklist

- ☐ 1. Walk around the decks checking for soft spots and investigate.

- ☐ 2. Check that the pushpit, pulpit, toe rail and deck fittings are secure and without the telltale signs of rust or rot around their base.

- ☐ 3. Check the stanchions for excessive movement. This could indicate a collision in the past.

- ☐ 4. Check that deck fittings like the capstan are secure and not leaking. They may need to be re-bedded.

- ☐ 5. Check for telltale signs of cracking around windlass and other highly stressed fittings.

- ☐ 6. Wooden boats: Check for rot wherever fresh water can lie – the cockpit corners, the hatch area, and scuppers etc.

- ☐ 7. Teak decking: Is the planking badly pitted around the grain? This indicates that it has been pressure washed.

- ☐ 8. Is the caulking sound or are there cracks along the edge of some planks that let in water?

- ☐ 9. Have dowel holes lost their cappings? Teak decks are very expensive to replace.

- ☐ 10. Check around hatches and windows. Are there water stains inside? If so, these will need to be re-bedded.

- ☐ 11. Capstan and deck winches: Do they turn easily? Do the ratchet pawls stick? These may need to be serviced.

Gas installation. Check for perished tubing and leaky connections. EU regulations insist that gas lockers must drain outboard of the hull.

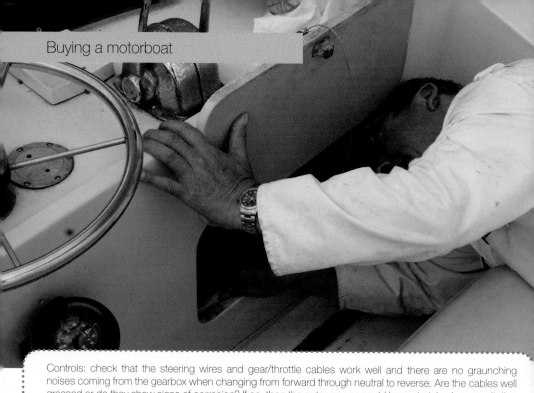

Controls: check that the steering wires and gear/throttle cables work well and there are no graunching noises coming from the gearbox when changing from forward through neutral to reverse. Are the cables well greased or do they show signs of corrosion? If so, then the outer covers could have stretched, necessitating complete replacement.

Check for any cracking especially in corners of the mouldings which could indicate stress problems. In this case, the damage has been caused by movement between the deck and coachroof mouldings. This is of no structural concern and simply needs to be refilled with resin paste, and gelled over.

Check that the anchor and windlass operate freely. The windlass operates under considerable load so check the through-deck fastenings are secure and do not leak.

97

Engines require regular maintenance to remain reliable. The state of the engine room and ancillary fittings provide a good indicator.

✓ Engineering Checklist

☐ 1. Does the engine have good water flow through it?

☐ 2. Check belts and hoses for cracks or wear. Rubber deteriorates quite quickly in a salty environment.

☐ 3. Check the oil in engine and transmission and rub a drop between your fingers. Can you feel any grit?

☐ 4. What is the colour? If it is grey or cream a water leak could have emulsified the oil.

☐ 5. How does it smell: burned? That is a sign of overheating. If in doubt, send a sample to a laboratory for testing.

☐ 6. Does the transmission shift easily or does it clunk?

☐ 7. Check for debris in the water strainers and pumps.

☐ 8. Test the seacocks to make sure they open and close.

☐ 9. Is the steering free and easy?

☐ 10. Check the electronic instruments, batteries and electrics, testing lights and pumps in turn.

☐ 11. Outboard and motors:

☐ i. Do they start easily?

☐ ii. Look for excessive corrosion under the cover and around the prop.

☐ iii. Check that the tilt mechanism works properly.

Check all skin fittings in turn for tell-tale signs of weeping and that they open and close easily.

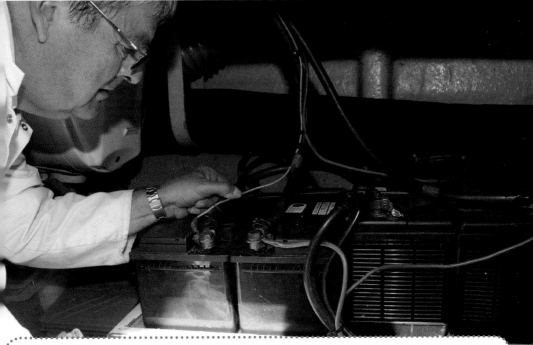

Batteries are expensive to replace. All boats should have at least two batteries – one for the boat's electrics, and one for starting the engine. Test the batteries for capacity and charge retention.

Check the oil in both the engine and gearbox. Any opaqueness or milkiness is a sure sign that there is a water leak somewhere. Does the oil smell 'burnt'? Rub some between your finger tips to check if the oil is carrying any deposits.

Look for signs of rust and weeping water around the engine, gearbox and stern gland. If you can't get a clear view, try to point a digital camera at the area and inspect the photographs for signs of corrosion and leaks.

Pull out the electrics panel and look for signs of wiring repairs. Check wiring runs beneath the floor and look for corrosion and any sign of 'blackness' at wiring ends. This will suggest that the wiring has been immersed at some point in the past.

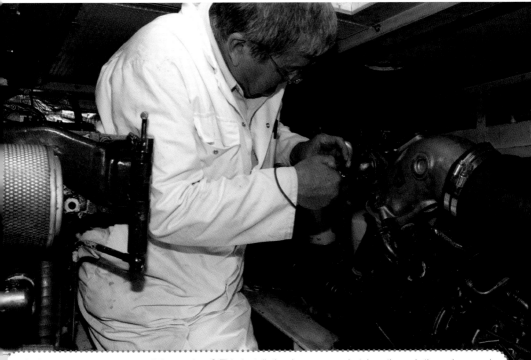

Is there easy access around the engines? This installation has access hatches through the saloon and cockpit floors and simplifies inspection and servicing considerably.

The insides of a yacht will provide clues to past history, repairs and potential problems.

☑ Inside Checklist

☐ 1. Is there a musty smell? This could indicate a leakage, water damage or general neglect.

☐ 2. Check the bilges for signs of damage or repair.

☐ 3. Wooden boats: Check each frame and bulkhead for cracking. These will need doublers to strengthen them.

☐ 4. Are there any waterlines inside the boat? Look for rust lines around the hull sides and engine. These indicate that the boat took on water or has been flooded in the past. Another give-away will be any wiring run below these waterlines. Disconnect their connections and check to see if the copper wiring has gone black.

☐ 5. Floors and bearers: Any sign of rot?

☐ 6. Are the handrails secure?

☐ 7. Is the upholstery in good shape?

☑ General Checklist

☐ 1. Check maintenance records for evidence of regular servicing. Look for recurring problems.

☐ 2. Contact previous owner(s) and ask about the boat.

☐ 3. Check the brokerage columns online and in magazines to determine value range for model and year.

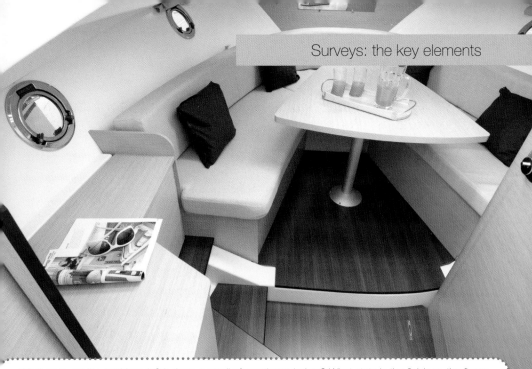

What state are the cushions in? Is there a smell of mustiness below? What state is the finish on the floors, treads and furnishings? These checks give a good indication on whether the boat has been well looked after.

The galley invariably gets the most wear and tear. Check the gas connections to the cooker and fridge are safe, the water pumps work satisfactorily and the water drains freely from the sink.

Pull the floors up and check for water in the bilge or waterlines that might suggest that the boat has been flooded in the past. Are the wooden bearers sound? Is anything loose in the bilge?

Look for any areas of delamination. This veneer damage around the forward hatch suggests that there is a long-standing leak. The hatch will need rebedding and the wooden trim replaced.

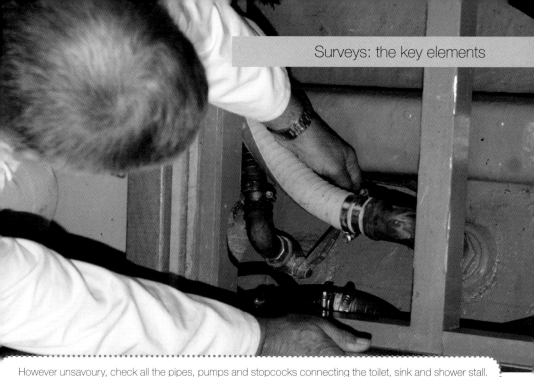

However unsavoury, check all the pipes, pumps and stopcocks connecting the toilet, sink and shower stall. If problems are hidden, this is where you are most likely to find them.

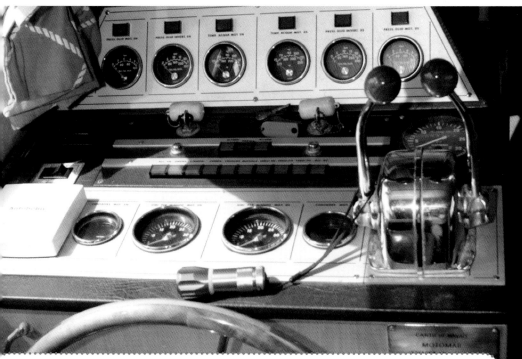

Inside the wheelhouse: If the vessel has twin steering positions, do the controls and instruments synchronise correctly with the second position on the flybridge or cockpit?

105

The trial

New boats

Once you have drawn up a shortlist of boats, book a trial sail on each and take detailed notes of what you like and dislike about each craft. Taking pictures of salient features will also act as an aide-memoire.

▶ Under power

How does she steer when going astern? Modern designs are expected to steer just as precisely going astern as they do in forward gear.

Once in open water, see how manoeuvrable she is going forward. Will she turn in her own length? Do this clockwise and anticlockwise: she is likely to turn tighter one way or the other depending on the action of the propeller. Boats with twin props can be turned in their own length simply by putting one engine in forward and the other astern.

How easy is she to dock? If bow and or stern thrusters are fitted, use them to manoeuvre alongside. If not, then docking under engines will be the best test to see how manoeuvrable she is under forward and reverse power alone.

Once you open the throttles, check to see how she performs into waves, even if this means returning across your own wake. The deeper the V-hull, the smoother she will cut through the waves.

Is there good visibility from the helm position – are there any blind spots?

How easy is it to walk around the deck – are there plenty of handholds?

How noisy are the engines – can you live with the level of decibels?

Is the engine and navigation instrumentation easy to read from the helm position?

Is the cockpit workable? If the boat is to be used for fishing you need plenty of clear space on both quarters.

Is the cockpit well sheltered and with coamings deep enough to stop anyone from falling overboard?

Is the cockpit self draining?

▶ Below decks

▼ These are the questions to ask yourself:

1. Do you like the layout?

2. Is the galley workable?

3. Are the berths comfortable?

4. How does the living area stack up?

5. Are there plenty of handholds throughout the boat?

6. Is there plenty of storage space?

7. How easy is it to access the engine compartment. Are the engine belts and fuel, oil and water filters all within easy reach?

▶ Taking delivery

Commissioning a new boat requires a detailed inspection of the boat, engineering and electronics to ensure that everything is just as you ordered – and working satisfactorily. If you lack experience, then call in a knowledgeable friend or surveyor to go through the boat with you. It could save you a lot of hassle and lost time on the water later while warranty work is completed.

▶ Sea trial

A trial run is imperative to check the inventory against your order, and that everything works satisfactorily. Ensure that you get a full tour of the vessel, taking in everything from steering to seacocks. Only when everything on your order sheet is ticked off should you hand over the final payment and sign the acceptance papers. The builder or agent will then present you with a builder's certificate, VAT receipt, an RCD compliance certificate, registration and warranty documents, and all the operating and service manuals for the vessel and its equipment.

Used boats

Testing a used boat is very similar to trialling a new vessel except that you are also looking for potential problems and wear and tear. Start by checking the engine exhaust. A lot a black smoke emitted at start up is a sure sign that fuel is not being burnt and indicates that, at best, the diesel engine needs a service, or worse, has blocked injectors or worn piston rings. And while you are looking, is there a good flow of cooling water coming out, or is it down to a trickle? The latter indicates a blockage, worn water pump or impeller.

Go through the Engineering Checklist on page 98.

▶ Deck

Check for general wear and tear. Any star crazing within the gel coat or cracks around the cockpit corners suggests stress or impact damage.

Go through the Deck Checklist on page 94.

▶ Inside

This is where wear and tear really shows. What are the state of the cushions and companion floors? If the interior has a 'tired' look about it, factor in the cost of having new cushions and headliners, and for giving paint and varnish work a facelift.

Go through the Inside and General Checklists on page 102.

Treat any survey report that the owner might offer on face value, because it is all too easy to remove any adverse comments. Insurance surveys are no better because these serve only to provide a valuation rather than a condition report on the boat.

▶ Making an offer

Always condition your offer with the term 'subject to survey'. Then, if problems are uncovered during closer inspection, the cost of repairs can be offset against the price you pay.

If the vessel is out of the water when you make an offer, make it conditional that you pay the final 10% balance after she has been launched and the engine has been run and tested satisfactorily.

RIPPLING SURF

Where to base her?

▶ What are the options?

If you live near the water, this question is academic, but if you are based more than an hour away, then you are likely to a have choice of harbours in which to base the boat. Spend a weekend or two scouting round by car to find the most suitable base.

▼ Things to consider:

1. Are there places within easy cruising distance to go to? It can become tedious covering the same patch of water each time.

2. What are the local facilities: fuel, lift-out, servicing etc?

3. What does the local boating club offer: club racing, organised cruises, mooring facilities, social activities?

4. Is the mooring within easy travelling distance from home? Is the route troubled by long queues during the season?

▶ Trailer boats

If you have space in the garden, the cheapest option is to keep the boat on its trailer at home. It is also often the most convenient, because if you have a spare hour or two you can easily tackle small maintenance jobs, or make some progress on a larger project.

The less time you spend getting to the water and setting up the boat, the more you will use her. Some marinas operate dry storage in a secure area, and will even launch the boat prior to your arrival, but think about the maintenance. If the boat is stored a long way from home, it simply won't get done, or only during good sailing time.

A motorboat being pulled off the dry-stack storage racks and launched at MDL's marina in Southampton, ready for her owner to step aboard.

▶ Launching/recovery

The big advantage of a trailer boat is that it gives you the opportunity to trail the boat to explore different cruising grounds and take her with you on family holidays both at home and abroad. But is she easy to launch and recover?

The first task is to locate a good slipway that you can launch and recover from at any state of the tide. The second is to have a good trailer preferably with a swinging cradle at the back end, which takes up the natural line of travel when the boat is launched and recovered. These are a quantum leap forward from early spine trailers and are designed so that the trailer wheel hubs and brakes need never be immersed in water. They not only simplify the whole process, but cut down on the maintenance and inevitable corrosion that leads to brake and hub failures.

The swing cradle reduces single-handed recovery to a simple routine. The trailer wheels need be immersed no deeper than the tyre rims, and with the boat's centre point close to the pivot point of the cradle, this rocks backwards, its rollers acting as a guide for the boat to slide off.

During recovery, the same rollers receive the bow and centre the boat, and as you winch in, the cradle tilts and these rollers then take up the line of the bilge as the keel is brought in line with the rollers set along the forward spine of the trailer. There is no risk of the boat moving off line and grazing the finish on the rollers. The wheel bearings are kept dry and the trauma of recovery becomes a thing of the past.

An Orkney Pilothouse 24 being recovered single-handedly on a swing cradle trailer, without the need to immerse the trailer in the water.

▶ Marina berth

A marina berth can be 2–3 times the cost of a swinging mooring, but does allow 24-hour access, free parking, electricity and water, together with a greater degree of security. There are invariably restaurants, toilets and showers nearby and it is much easier to entertain guests onboard. If time is limited, then the extra cost may well be worth considering.

▼ Things to consider:

1. What are the tidal restrictions to getting in and out of the basin?

2. Is the water polluted?

3. Is there plenty of parking space?

4. How noisy are the neighbours?

▶ Pile mooring

Pile moorings have been introduced in crowded anchorages to maximise the number of boats that can be accommodated in a small area. They are more secure than swinging from a buoy because the boats are attached fore and aft to the piles. They are invariably more expensive than a swinging mooring.

Some harbours operate a water taxi, which can simplify getting to and from the yacht, but does it operate during weekdays and out of season? There is nothing more boring for friends and family, than standing around for an hour or so waiting idly for one person to put the yacht back on its mooring and row ashore – especially after a long day of sailing.

▶ Non-tidal waterside mooring

Permanent moorings on the canal or river banks are greatly sought after.

▼ Things to consider:

1. Does the public have free access along the tow path?

2. Is there any security or CCTV cameras?

3. Does the stretch of water have a history of draught or flooding?

4. Is the area sheltered from the prevailing winds?

5. Are the tie points on the bank strong enough to hold the weight of your vessel?

Paperwork

▶ **What paperwork do I need to carry?**

Ship's papers

These must all be original documents (photocopies are not acceptable), and comprise:

▶ Registration document

This is compulsory if you intend to take a non-commercial pleasure craft outside UK territorial waters. This applies both to boats that are sailed or driven to a foreign port, or trailered on the road by train or ferry.

▶ Proof of ownership

A bill of sale is required for vessels registered on the UK Small Ships Register (SSR) because this register only indicates the vessel's nationality, and not ownership of the vessel. If the owner is not onboard, the skipper is required to carry a letter authorising use of the vessel to prove that the loan is not an illegal charter arrangement.

▶ Proof of VAT status

Residents of the EU can only use vessels within Community waters if VAT has been paid or 'deemed' to have been paid. Proof of the VAT status of a vessel is not part of the ship's papers, so it is required in order to prove that the boat is entitled to free movement throughout the EU. If documentary evidence is not readily available in the form of a receipted invoice or similar, customs officials have the power to impound your boat, so be warned.

▶ Recreational Craft Compliant

If your vessel was built or imported into the EU, including Iceland, Liechtenstein, Norway and Switzerland after 16th June 1998, you are required to carry proof that your boat is Recreational Craft Directing (RCD) compliant. This requirement is satisfied by the Builder's CE mark, shown on the manufacturer's plate, which certifies that a product has met EU consumer safety, health and environmental requirements.

▶ Ship Radio Licence

Under the International Radio Regulations, vessels with any kind of radio transmitter, even a hand-held VHF, must have a licence. Ofcom issues the licence in the UK, and applications can be made online at www.ofcom.org.uk. The licence details the equipment onboard, and covers:

▼ Ship Radio Licence should include:

1. Fixed or portable VHF or VHF/DSC radio
2. MF/HF radio equipment
3. AIS transponder
4. Emergency Position Indicating Radio Beacon (EPIRB)
5. Personal Locator Beacon (PLB)
6. Radar
7. Satellite communications
8. Search and Rescue Transponder (SART)
9. Ship Earth Station (SES) equipment

Check if your set has an Active Radar Target Enhancer or is ATIS capable, since these are not available to select on the list of licensable equipment and you need to request a variation to your Ship Radio Licence. The licence has to be updated whenever changes are made to the equipment onboard.

Call signs and Maritime Mobile Service Identity (MMSI) numbers are allocated when the first application is made. This call sign remains valid for the lifetime of the vessel regardless of changes in ownership or name, unless the boat is sold outside the UK.

MMSI numbers are only issued when Digital Selective Calling (DSC) and/or Ship Earth Station (SES) equipment is fitted.

Remember that EPIRBs must be registered both on the Ship Radio Licence and with the MCA EPIRB Registry to ensure that all Maritime Rescue Co-ordination Centres (MRCC) have the necessary information should your EPIRB be activated.

▶ European inland waterways

Under the Regional Arrangement Concerning the Radiotelephone Service on Inland Waterways (RAINWAT), all vessels navigating the inland waterways of central Europe must be equipped with a VHF radio with an active ATIS transmission facility. An ATIS number is issued by Ofcom as a Notice of Variation to the Ship Radio Licence. For the moment, Ofcom does this manually, and applicants must allow up to a month for details of the vessel to be activated by the European regulator, the Belgian Institute for Post and Telecommunications (BIPT).

The Ofcom website (www.ofcom.org.uk) provides answers to FAQs about ATIS and RAINWAT. It also explains how to request the Notice of Variation to your Ship Radio Licence and obtain the ATIS number for your vessel. You must also carry a copy of the Basel Arrangement governing ATIS onboard. This can be downloaded from the RAINWAT website, www.rainwat.bipt.be.

▶ Hand-held radio

The Ship Portable Radio Licence is only valid in UK waters. Licensees voyaging within RAINWAT countries must apply for a full Ship Radio Licence. If your vessel does not have an MMSI number, then you can obtain one by emailing licensingcentre@ofcom.org.uk.

Digital Selective Calling (DSC) VHF radio transmitters are not yet mandatory aboard small pleasure craft in UK waters, but new small craft VHF sets are now Global Maritime Distress Safety System (GMDSS) compatible, though with some, the DSC element has to be purchased separately. DSC is a tone signalling system similar to the tone dialling on your phone, operating on VHF Channel 70. It has the ability to include other information such as the vessel's identification number, the purpose of the call, your position, the channel you want to speak on – and when necessary, the nature of distress.

The distress message is repeated automatically every 4 minutes until acknowledged either by a Coastguard station or ship within radio range.

The minimum standard for small craft DSC-equipped radios for fixed use in Europe is EN 301 025. Check that the equipment is marked in accordance with the EU Radio and Telecommunications Terminal Equipment (R&TTE).

▶ Radio Operator's Certificate

A VHF radio may be used by anyone in emergency situations, but can only be used for general transmissions by a licensed operator or person under the direct supervision of someone with a Maritime Radio Operator's Certificate.

The Short Range Certificate (SRC) covering the use of VHF/DSC equipment is the common operator's certificate for cruising vessels. You must attend a day-long course at a sailing school or club to gain the certificate.

A Long Range Certificate (LRC) is required for MF, HF and satellite communications equipment. The LRC is administered by the Association of Marine Electronic and Radio Colleges (AMERC). Courses range from 3–4 days and include an examination, which you must pass to gain the certificate.

This powerboat ran up on the rocks while under auto-pilot. Her skipper had nodded off and there was no one else on watch. He had a radio to call for assistance.

▶ Marine insurance

Your home insurance policy may include coverage for low value boats, but the coverage is often very limited. Typically, a home insurance policy will pay up to £1,000 if something happens to your boat while it is at your house and may even offer some liability coverage while you are using the boat, but the coverage is likely to be less than ideal.

Marine insurance premiums can vary widely, but on the basis that you pay for what you get, the cheaper policies carry a greater number of exclusions and 'extras'. If you have any doubts, use an independent insurance broker to source the best cover.
Yachts older than 15 years are usually insured on an 'agreed value' basis and in the event of a total loss, will pay out the full amount.

Uninsured cover will cover you in the event of damage caused by another vessel that is uninsured. Another value clause to look for is legal fees in the event of a dispute. When my yacht sank during its relaunch following a winter refit, while in the hands of the marina operator, the legal team associated with my insurance company secured an £18,000 settlement. The extra cost on the policy was just £11 – money well spent!

If you suffer a partial loss, damaged items are usually replaced on a new-for-old basis. Marine insurance should also cover hurricane and tornado damage, though the policy may stipulate layup during those periods. Liability coverage protects you against 3rd party claims for damage and injury to someone other than you or a family member. In a world where no-win no-fee lawsuits are now common, it pays to have this coverage.

▶ Geographical issues

If you are cruising extensively check that your policy covers the areas you want to sail to. Yachts based in the UK for instance, often have a latitude restriction limiting you to a cruising area south of the River Elbe and north of La Rochelle. In the Caribbean, insurance companies insist that vessels are laid up or moored in secure anchorages during the hurricane season – June 1 to November 30. Pirates operate in many parts of the world and you may have difficulty securing insurance in these waters. Consider crew medical and liability insurance. It may be cheaper to include this in the boat insurance plan.

Personal papers

▶ Passport

Each crew member must carry a passport. The crew may also require visas if you intend to cruise outside EU waters. Check well ahead of time because visas can take several days to get. If you have a non-EU citizen onboard, they will need to clear through immigration each time you cross from one country to another, even if the vessel is not required to clear customs.

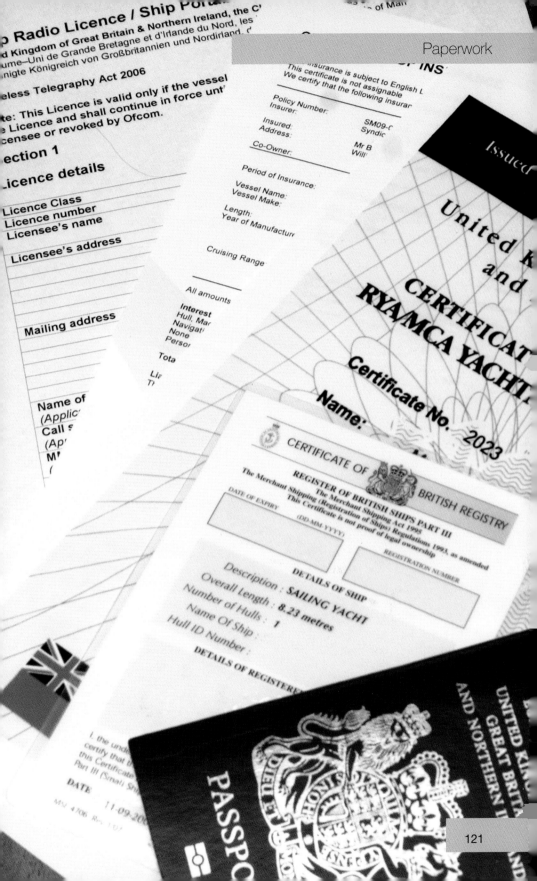

p Radio Licence / Ship Por

d Kingdom of Great Britain & Northern Ireland, the C
ume–Uni de Grande Bretagne et d'Irlande du Nord, les
nigte Königreich von Großbritannien und Nordirland,

eless Telegraphy Act 2006

te: This Licence is valid only if the vessel
e Licence and shall continue in force unt
censee or revoked by Ofcom.

ection 1

Licence details

Licence Class
Licence number
Licensee's name

Licensee's address

Mailing address

Name of
(Applic
Call s
(Ap
M
(

INS

insurance is subject to English L
This certificate is not assignable
We certify that the following insuran

Policy Number:
Insurer:

Insured: SM09-C
Address: Syndic

Co-Owner: Mr B
                                      Will

Period of Insurance:

Vessel Name:
Vessel Make:

Length:
Year of Manufactur

Cruising Range

All amounts

Interest
Hull, Mar
Navigati
None
Persor

Tota

Li
T

Issued

United K
and
CERTIFICAT
RYA/MCA YACHT.

Certificate No. 2023

Name:

CERTIFICATE OF BRITISH REGISTRY

REGISTER OF BRITISH SHIPS PART III
The Merchant Shipping Act 1995
The Merchant Shipping (Registration of Ships)
This Certificate (Registration of Ships) Regulations 1993, as amended
is not proof of legal ownership

DATE OF EXPIRY
(DD-MM-YYYY)

REGISTRATION NUMBER

DETAILS OF SHIP

Description : SAILING YACHT
Overall Length : 8.23 metres
Number of Hulls : 1
Name Of Ship :
Hull ID Number :

DETAILS OF REGISTER

I, the und
certify that th
this Certificate
Part III (Small Sh

DATE   11-09-200

MSF 4706 R

UNITED KING
GREAT BRIT
AND NORTHERN IR

PASSPO

▶ International Certificate of Competence (ICC)

Whilst it is not (yet) a requirement for UK skippers of pleasure craft below 24m (78.74ft) or 80 tonnes to have a certificate of competence or licence, this is not the same in all EU countries. The requirements vary from country to country so you need to check out what is required in advance. You can do this through the country's National Sailing Authority or embassy.

If you do not hold a Yachtmaster certificate and are chartering a vessel or cruising in Northern Europe, a letter from a Flag Officer or Club Secretary outlining your experience and competence may suffice. However, skippers of UK flagged vessels are required to hold an ICC when cruising the inland waterways of Europe and inland and coastal waters of Mediterranean countries. Certainly, anyone planning to charter abroad should ask the charter company for details of the certification they require to meet local laws and insurance requirements. The ICC is NOT a qualification. It is simply documentary assurance from one government to another that the holder meets locally accepted levels of competence. It allows UK citizens and residents to navigate pleasure craft in the waters of participating states without the need to comply with national transport laws, in particular, compulsory certification requirements.

▶ European Inland Waterways

In addition to holding an ICC, you must also learn the Code Européen des Voies de la Navigation Intérieure (CEVNI) which governs navigation on the interconnected European inland waterways. You will need to pass a short multiple-choice exam at a recognised sailing school.

▶ How do I apply for an ICC or CEVNI?

The Royal Yachting Association (RYA) is the UK issuing authority for the ICC and CEVNI endorsement. To prove your competence to gain an ICC you must have attained an RYA practical training certificate in either the Radio Operation or First Aid categories. Remember that the ICC is valid only for the type of vessel and level that you passed your competence test on. The minimum age is 16.

e-Borders – what new EU legislation could mean to you

The aim of new e-Borders legislation is to collect and analyse information about everyone intending to travel to or from the United Kingdom before they leave in order to provide the Security Services with a comprehensive record of everyone crossing UK borders.

The legislation, requiring all cruising folk to file the equivalent of a 'flight plan' listing crew details and intended destination, every time you set out from your marina berth or mooring, was due to come into force at the end of 2010. However, a government report questioned the legality of the e-Borders programme as it would cut across the overriding principle of EU residents having the right to travel freely within the entire EU. So the current leaky border controls will continue until someone comes up with a brighter plan. However, you still need to have all your vessel and crew paperwork in order, even though the sole interest for 9 out of 10 harbour officials remains focused on how you are going to pay for the berthing facilities.

▼ Course certificate requirement	ICC may be issued for			
	Power		Inland Waters	Coastal waters
	up to 10m	up to 24m	CEVNI test required	
1. National Powerboat Certificate (non tidal) Level 2 or above	✓		✓	
2. National Powerboat Certificate (tidal) Level 2 or above	✓		✓	✓
3. Helmsman's Course Completion Certificate		✓	✓	✓
4. Inland Waterways Helmsman Certificate		✓	✓	✓
5. Day Skipper Practical Course Completion Certificate (Power)		✓	✓	✓
6. Day Skipper Practical Course Completion Certificate (Sail)	✓		✓	✓
7. Coastal Skipper Practical Course Completion Certificate (Power)		✓	✓	✓
8. Coastal Skipper Practical Course Completion Certificate (Sail)	✓		✓	✓
9. MCA Deck Officer Certificate of Competence (any grade)		✓	✓	✓
10. RN, Army or RAF Bridge Watchkeeping Certificate	✓		✓	✓
11. MCA or Local Authority Boatman's Licence		✓	✓	✓
12. MCA Boatmaster Certificate		✓	✓	✓
13. RYA Dinghy Instructor and National Powerboat Certificate Level 2 or higher		✓	✓	✓
14. Personal Watercraft Proficiency Certificate		✓	✓	✓
15. Coastal Skipper Practical Course Completion Certificate (Power)	✓		✓	✓

Training and qualifications

For the moment at least, there is no legal requirement for anyone in the UK to undergo training before taking a boat out on their own, though in some other EU countries, skippers are required to hold a certificate of competence.

That said, every skipper is legally responsible not just for the safety of their crew, but the actions they take afloat, so it makes good sense for everyone in the family to undergo some formal training.

The Royal Yachting Association (RYA) has a syllabus of courses from the introductory Level 1 for complete novices through to Yachtmaster certification. You can use them simply to increase your knowledge and confidence, or as a progression to the RYA/MCA Certificates of Competence (ICC).

Motorboat courses

▶ Level 1

A short introduction to Motorboating for complete beginners. By the end of the course you will be able to launch and recover a boat from a road trailer, understand everyday boat handling as well as the use of safety equipment.

Pre-course experience:	None
Assumed knowledge:	None
Minimum duration:	1 day
Minimum age:	8 Candidates under the age of 16 will be issued with an endorsed certificate.
Course content:	Launch and recovery (8–11 year olds observe) Preparation of boat and crew, boat handling, picking up and securing to a mooring buoy, leaving and coming alongside, being towed.
Ability after the course:	Able to drive a motorboat under supervision.

▶ Helmsman

A two-day course for skippers as well as crews, covering basic boat handling, engine checks and safety.

Pre-course experience:	None
Assumed knowledge:	None
Minimum duration:	2 days
Minimum age:	12
Course content:	Boat preparation, boat handling, types of craft, engines and drives, engine operation and maintenance, safety and seamanship, rules of the road, securing to a buoy, berthing alongside, man overboard recovery.
Ability after the course:	Competent to handle a motor cruiser of a specific type in sheltered waters.

▶ Day Skipper

A course for skippers with some experience of basic navigation and boat handling skills. You will learn to skipper a short passage with the instructor on hand to give advice and ensure your safety. You will experience being in charge, taking credit when everything goes well and being responsible when it doesn't. This course will also help you get the best from electronic aids like GPS and radar.

Pre-course experience:	2 days practical experience on a motor cruiser.
Assumed knowledge:	Basic navigation and helmsmanship. It is recommended that you attend the Day Skipper Shorebased Course beforehand.
Minimum duration:	4 days
Minimum age:	16
Course content:	Preparation for sea, boat handling, navigation, pilotage, passage making, meteorology, rules of the road, engines, emergency situations, night cruising.
Ability after the course:	Able to skipper a motorboat.

▶ Coastal Skipper

The Coastal Skipper course provides the knowledge to skipper a motorboat on limited coastal cruises. The exam includes an assessment of your skippering skills, boat handling, general seamanship, navigation, safety awareness and knowledge of the IRPCS (collision regulations), meteorology and signals. Candidates are set tasks to demonstrate their ability and questioned on any part of the syllabus for all practical and shore-based courses.

Pre-course experience:	15 days, 2 days as skipper, 300 miles, 8 night hours.
Assumed knowledge:	Boat handling to the standard of the Day Skipper practical motor cruising course and navigation to the standard of the Coastal Skipper/Yachtmaster shore based course.
Minimum duration:	5 days
Minimum age:	17
Course content:	Passage planning, preparation for sea, pilotage, passage making and ability as a skipper, radar, boat handling, adverse weather conditions, emergency situations.
Ability after the course:	Able to skipper a motor cruiser on coastal passages by day and night.

▶ Yachtmaster

The Yachtmaster is competent to skipper a motorboat on any passage and the certificate of competence is recognised worldwide. There is no formal training course leading up to the exam, but some sailing schools do run a combined training course and examination.

▶ Yachtmaster Coastal exam pre-requisites

The exam includes an assessment of your skippering skills, boat handling, general seamanship, navigation, safety awareness and knowledge of the IRPCS, meteorology and signals.

Minimum seatime:	30 days, 2 days as skipper, 800 miles, 12 night hours (if you hold the Coastal Skipper course certificate this is reduced to 20 days, 2 days as skipper, 400 miles, 12 night hours). Half the qualifying sea time must be conducted in tidal waters.
Form of exam:	Practical
Certification required:	A restricted (VHF only) Radio Operators Certificate or a GMDSS Short Range Certificate or higher grade of marine radio certificate. A valid first aid certificate (first aid qualifications held by Police, Fire and Armed Services are acceptable).
Minimum exam duration:	6–10 hours for 1 candidate, 8–14 hours for 2 candidates.
Minimum age:	17

▶ Yachtmaster conversion between sail and power

Holders of the Yachtmaster Coastal or Yachtmaster Offshore Sail certificates of competence can take a conversion exam to obtain the equivalent power certificates.

Exam duration:	3 hours. The examiner will concentrate on those sections within the syllabus that are markedly different in a motor cruiser, including boat handling, passage planning and radar, etc.
Pre-exam requirements:	The mileage must be in the type of boat that you are converting to. All qualifying sea time must be within 10 years prior to the exam. Half of the qualifying sea time must have been conducted in tidal waters.

 For Yachtmaster Coastal conversion exams

1. **Minimum of 400 miles**

2. **12 days living on board**

3. **2 days as skipper**

4. **12 night hours**

 For Yachtmaster Offshore conversion exams

1. **Minimum of 1,250 miles**

2. **25 days living on board**

3. **3 days as skipper**

4. **3 passages over 60 miles including 1 overnight and 1 as skipper**

DWD Marine forecast:
weather.mailasail.com

International Institute of Marine Surveying: www.iims.org.uk
Helpline: +44 (0)23 9238 5223

British Marine Federation:
www.britishmarine.co.uk
Helpline: +44 (0)1784 473377

HM Revenue and Customs:
www.hmrc.gov.uk
National helpline: +44 (0)845 010 9000
National yachtline: +44 (0)845 723 1110

Maritime and Coastguard Agency:
www.dft.gov.uk/mca
Emergency tel: 999

Met Office: www.metoffice.gov.uk
National helpline: +44 (0)870 900 0100
From overseas:+44 (0)1392 885680

Ofcom Radio Licensing Centre:
www.ofcom.org.uk/licensing
National helpline: +44 (0)20 7981 3131
E-mail: licensing centre@ofcom.org.uk

Register of British Ships:
www.mcga.gov.uk
National helpline: +44 (0)29 2044 8813

Royal Yachting Association (RYA):
www.rya.org.uk
National helpline:+44 (0)845 345 0400

UK Border Agency:
www.bia.homeoffice.gov.uk
National helpline: +44 (0)845 010 5200
E-mail:
ukbanationalityenquiries@ukba.gsi.gov.uk

UK Hydrographic Office:
www.ukho.gov.uk
National helpline: +44 (0)1823 284077
Notices to mariners:
noticestomariners@ukho.gov.uk

Sailing Directions:
+44 (0)1823 337900 ext 3382
E-mail: sailingdirections@ukho.gov.uk

Tides helpline:
+44 (0)1823 337900 ext 3533/3530
E-mail: tides@ukho.gov.uk

Motorboat charter companies

Charter World LLP:
www.charterworld.com
National helpline: +44 (0)20 7193 7830

Hoseasons:
www.hoseasons.co.uk
National helpline: +44 (0)844 847 1115

The Moorings: www.moorings.co.uk
National helpline: +44 (0)844 463 6879

Motorboat time-share companies

The Cruising Association:
www.cruising.org.uk
Tel: +44 (0)20 7537 2828

Flexisail: www.flexisail.com
Tel: +44 (0)1590 688008

The Moorings: www.moorings.co.uk
National helpline: +44 (0)844 463 6879

Finance companies

CGI Finance: www.cgi-finance.co.uk

Close Marine Finance:
www.closemarine.com
Tel: +44 (0)208 399 1111

Diamond Finance:
www.diamondvf.co.uk
National helpline: +44 (0)845 166 2316

HSBC: www.business.hsbc.co.uk
National helpline: +44 (0)800 085 52851

Lombard Finance: www.lombard.co.uk
Tel: +44 (0)238 023 2171

Norton Finance:
www.nortonfinance.co.uk
National helpline: +44 (0)800 694 4400

Glossary

A

ABAFT – Behind or towards the stern.

ABEAM – At right angles to the boat.

AFT – See Abaft.

AIS – Automatic Identifying System.

AMIDSHIPS – Centre of the boat.

ANAEROBIC – Corrosion or rot in which there is no dissolved oxygen present such as when water is trapped under a fitting.

ANCHOR – Device to moor the yacht in open water on the end of a line.

ANEMOMETER – Instrument to measure wind speed.

ANODE – Sacrificial zinc or magnesium blocks attached to the hull to protect dissimilar metals from galvanic or electronic corrosion.

ANTIFOULING – Paint containing toxic chemicals to discourage growth of weed and marine life.

ATHWARTSHIPS – From one side of the vessel to the other.

B

BAILER – Scoop to remove water from inside the boat.

BEAM – Mid part of the boat, or measurement of maximum width of the hull.

BEAM SHELF – Structural member inside the hull to support the beams.

BEARING – Compass direction.

BECKET – A second eye or attachment point in a pulley block.

BERTH – A place to sleep; permanent mooring.

BIGHT – An open loop in a rope.

BILGE – Bottom inside part of the hull.

BLISTERING – Coating defect caused by physical or chemical instability.

BLOCK – A pulley.

BLOCK AND TACKLE – A multi-purchase pulley system.

BOLLARD – Vertical post on a quayside to make fast mooring lines.

BOOT-TOP – Decorative band around the waterline.

BOW – Front end of the boat.

BOWLINE – A knot used to tie a loop into the end of a rope.

BOW ROLLER – Roller device to run anchor chain over the bow.

BOWSPRIT – Spar that extends forward of the bow.

BOW THRUSTER – Power unit running transverse through the bow to assist manoeuvring.

BREAKWATER – Small upstanding ledge or coaming across the foredeck to deflect water.

BROACH – When a boat slews out of control broadside to the wind and sea.

BRONZE – Copper/tin alloy used to cast fittings.

BULLSEYE – Wooden block or thimble with a hole drilled through it to take a rope to act as a block or stopper.

BULKHEAD – Transverse partition within the boat.

BUNG – Plug to block a drainage hole.

BUOY – Floating racing mark or navigation mark.

BUOYANCY – Power to float, having a density less than water.

BURGEE – Small flag flown from the masthead.

C

CABLE – Chain or rope attached to anchor.

CAM CLEAT – Cleat with two spring-load cams to hold a rope.

CAMBER – Curvature of a sail.

CALORIFIER – Heating system for a water tank.

CAPSIZE – Point when a boat tips over.

CAPSTAN – Winch to haul in the anchor chain.

CARLINE – Structural member to strengthen an opening within the deck.

CATAMARAN – Twin-hulled vessel.

CATHEDRAL HULL – Triple V-shaped hull.

CATHODE – Positive anode to limit electronic action between dissimilar metals under water.

CE CERTIFICATION – Certificate confirming that vessel complies with EU Directives.

CENTRE OF BUOYANCY – Point where the buoyant force of water acts on the hull.

CHAIN PLATE – Strong mounting point on the hull to attach mast stays.

CHART – Map of the sea.

CHINE – Line or crease in the hull. A hull built from flat sheets of plywood is known as a hard chine boat.

CLEAR ASTERN / CLEAR AHEAD – One boat is clear astern of another when her hull and equipment in normal position are behind a line abeam from the after most point of the other boat's hull and equipment in normal position. The other boat is clear ahead.

CLEAT – Fitting designed to hold a rope under tension without the use of a knot or hitch.

CLINKER CONSTRUCTION – Traditional form of hull construction where the planks overlap each other.

CLOVE HITCH – Common knot or hitch used to tie a rope to a ring or rail.

COAMING – Small upstanding ledge or breakwater across or around the deck to deflect water.

COCKPIT – Area of the boat where helm and crew operate the boat.

COACHROOF – Raised section of deck forming a cabin.

COAMING – Breakwater to protect the cockpit.

COCKPIT – Control area within the boat.

COL REGS – International regulations for the prevention of collision at sea.

COMPANIONWAY – Main passage through the boat.

COMPASS – Navigation instrument that points to the magnetic north pole.

COMPLETION – Official delivery date.

CORE – Lightweight material sandwiched between structural membranes of the hull and deck.

COUNTER – Area of deck between cockpit and transom.

CQR – Type of anchor shaped like a plough.

CUTLASS BEARING – Water lubricated bearing supporting the outer end of the propeller shaft.

CURRENT – A stream of water.

D

DECK HEAD – Cabin ceiling.

DEPRESSION – Meteorological term for an area of low pressure.

DEVIATION – Compass error influenced by magnetic materials nearby.

DINGHY – Small open boat without a fixed keel.

DISPLACEMENT – Volume/weight that a hull displaces in water.

DODGERS – Cloth spray protector attached to the guard rails or lifelines.

DORADE – Self draining deck ventilator.

DORY – Open, stable, sea going dinghy or tender.

DOWNWIND – Moving in the same direction as the wind.

DRAFT – The depth of water that a vessel draws.

E

EBB – Outgoing tide or flow.

EDDIES – Area of reverse or back-running current.

ENSIGN – National flag flown from the staff on the stern of a vessel.

EPOXY – Strong synthetic resin or coating.

F

FAIRWAY – Main navigable channel.

FAIR WIND – Wind direction that allows a boat to sail from A to B without tacking.

FATHOM – Nautical unit of measure equal to 6ft (1.828m).

FENDER – Portable cushion or inflatable bladder to protect the hull from rubbing against another boat or a pontoon.

FERRO-CEMENT – Concrete construction reinforced by a steel frame.

FIDDLE – Raised edge or rail around stove or table.

FLARE – Pyrotechnic used to signal an emergency; shape of hull where it curves outwards from centreline.

FLOOD TIDE – A rising tide.

FLOOR – Structural member in the bottom of hull.

FOLLOWING WIND – Opposite of headwind, when the wind comes from astern.

FORE, FORWARD – Front part of hull.

FOREDECK – Front end of deck.

FOTHERING – The process of stuffing anything that comes to hand (eg sleeping bags) into a hole in the boat to stop water ingress.

FREEBOARD – Height of a boat's side above the water.

FRP – Fibre reinforced plastic.

G

GALLEY – Kitchen area within a boat.

GALVANIC ACTION – Electrolytic corrosion between two dissimilar metals.

GALVANIZED – Zinc coating to protect steel.

GARBOARD – Hull planking adjacent to keel.

GEL COAT – The smooth waterproof outer resin coating of a fibre-reinforced moulded hull and deck.

GPS – Satellite-based global positioning system.

GREY WATER – Waste water.

GRP – Glass reinforced plastic.

GUARD RAIL – Safety lines or lifelines running around the side decks.

GUDGEON – Female part of a pair of rudder hangings into which the male pintle fits.

GUNWALE – Outer strengthening piece around the top of the hull.

H

HALF HITCH – Temporary knot to attach a rope to a rail.

HALYARD – Rope or wire line to hoist sails up the mast.

HARD CHINE – Line where the flat sheets used to construct a hull meet.

HAWSE PIPE – Tube through deck leading anchor cable to chain locker.

HEADS – Marine toilet, compartment.

HEADING – Direction that a boat is taking.

HEAD TO WIND – Boat facing directly into wind – the no-go zone.

HEAVE TO – To bring the boat to a halt, head to wind.

HELM – Rudder. Also short for helmsman or helmsperson.

HITCH – Type of knot for attaching a rope to a rail or hoop.

HOLDING TANK – Sewage tank.

HOVE TO – See Heave to.

I

INGLEFIELD CLIPS – Interlocking C-shaped clips used to attach signal flaps.

INBOARD/OUTDRIVE – Inboard engine attached to a transom mounted steerable drive.

INVENTORY – List of equipment supplied with a yacht.

INVERTER – Electrical device to convert direct current (DC) to alternating current (DC).

J

JACKSTAY – A strong webbing strap running the length of the boat on each side. By clipping the lifeline to this, it ensures that Jack stays on the boat.

JETTY – A structure extending out from harbour wall or beach on which to moor a vessel.

K

KEDGE – Light, temporary anchor to hold the boat against an adverse tidal stream.

KEEL – Structural backbone of vessel.

KEELSON – Structural member to which iron or lead keel is attached.

KING PLANK – Main structural plank running down the centreline of the foredeck.

KNEE – Supporting structure between transverse beams and side of hull.

KNOT – Nautical mile per hour (1 nautical mile equals 1.15 statute miles or 1,852m). Also refers to a rope tie.

KNUCKLE – Sharp longitudinal line of distortion within the hull.

L

LAMINATE – Layers of fibre reinforced plastic embedded in resin; decorative surface finish.

LANYARD – Short length of cord used as a safety line..

LAZARETTE – Stern locker.

LEAD – The direction that a rope is led.

LEE CLOTH – Cloth divider to prevent crew from falling out of their bunk.

LEE SHORE – Shoreline which the wind is blowing towards.

LEEWARD – Opposite of windward; away from the wind.

LIFE JACKET – Buoyancy vest designed to keep a nonswimmer or unconscious person floating head up.

LIMBER HOLE – drainage hole within the bilge.

LOA – Length overall.

LWL – Load waterline or length of waterline.

M

MAGNETIC NORTH – Compass heading.

MAGNETIC VARIATION – Difference in angle between True North and Magnetic North.

MARK – An object (buoy) the sailing instructions require a boat to pass on a specified side.

MAST – A spar going straight up from the deck, used to attach sail and boom.

MARLIN HITCH – Line of linked knots tying sail to a spar.

MIDSHIPS – The middle part of the vessel.

MULTIHULL – Generic term for a catamaran or trimaran.

MY – Prefix for name of vessel meaning Motor Yacht.

N

NAUTICAL ALMANAC – Annual publication listing tide tables, lights and radio beacons.

NAUTICAL MILE – 1 nautical mile equals 1.15 statute miles or 1,852m.

NEAP TIDES – Tides with the smallest rise and fall. Opposite of spring tides.

O

OAR – Wooden blade to row or scull a boat with.

OBSTRUCTION – An object that a boat cannot pass without changing course substantially to avoid it, eg the shore, perceived underwater dangers or shallows.

OCCULTING LIGHT – Flashing navigation light where the period of light is longer than the period of darkness.

OFFSHORE WIND – Wind blowing seaward off the land.

ONSHORE WIND – Wind blowing inland off the sea.

OSMOSIS – Water penetration beneath the gel coat on a fibre reinforced moulding.

OUTBOARD MOTOR – Self contained propulsion system that bolts to the transom of a boat.

P

P-BRACKET – Bracket containing cutlass bearing, supporting the outer end of the prop shaft.

PAINTER – Mooring line.

PASSARELLE – Gang plank linking dock to aft deck.

PELICAN HOOK – Metal hook with a cam-action lock.

PFD – Personal flotation device such as a buoyancy aid or life jacket.

PINTLE – Male part of a pair of rudder hangings that fits into the female gudgeon.

PITCH – Theoretical distance that a propeller will move a vessel forward with one revolution.

PLANING – When a boat lifts its bows out of the water, and because of the reduced drag, then accelerates onto a planing attitude.
PORT – Left hand side of a boat.
PURCHASE – Mechanical advantage of the block and tackle or lever.
PUSHPIT – Safety guardrail around the stern.

Q

QUARTER – Sides of the boat aft, ie starboard quarter, port quarter.
QUARTER BERTH – single berths within the end of the hull.

R

RACE – Fast running tide or stream.
RADAR – Navigation device used to determine angle and range of coastline and other vessels.
RADAR REFLECTOR – Reflector to enhance radar signals transmitted by other vessels.
RAKE – Degree that a mast leans back from vertical.
RCD – Recreational Craft Directive.
REEF KNOT – Knot joining two ropes together.
RHUMB LINE – Straight line between two points drawn on a Mercator chart.
RIDING TURN – When a rope or sheet crosses under itself and jams, most often around a winch.
RIG – General term for mast, spars and sails.
RIGGING – Standing wires that hold up the mast.
RIGGING SCREW – Screw to tension shrouds. Also known as a bottle screw.
RIGHT OF WAY – Term within Collision Regulations denoting a boat with rights, as opposed to a boat that must give way.
ROCKER – Fore and aft curve within the central underside sections of the boat.
ROUND TURN AND TWO HALF HITCHES – Knot used to attach rope to a rail or hoop.
ROWLOCK – Swivel fitting on the gunwale to cradle a rowing oar.
RUBBING STRAKE – A strengthening strip secured to the gunwale as a protective buffer.
RUDDER – Moving foil to steer the boat with.

S

SEA BREEZE – Onshore wind opposite to a land breeze, that develops when the temperature of the land is higher than the sea.
SELF BAILER – Thru-hull bailer that, once activated, allows the bilge water to flow out when the keel boat is planing.
SEACOCK – A valve going through the hull, which can be shut from inside the boat.
SEXTANT – A navigational instrument used to determine the vertical position of an object such as the sun, moon or stars. Used with celestial navigation.
SHACKLE – Metal link with screw pin to connect wires and lines.
SHEER – Line where topsides meet the deck.
SHEAVE – The wheel within a block
SHEEPSHANK – Knot used to shorten a rope.
SHEET BEND – Knot used to join two dissimilar sized ropes together.
SHOCK CORD – Elastic or bungee cord made of rubber strands.
SHROUDS – Wires supporting either side of the mast.
SKEG – Short fin projecting from the bottom of vessel at the stern.
SLIP HITCH – A temporary knot used to secure sails.
SLIP LINE – Temporary double line with both ends made fast to the boat that can be released from onboard and pulled in.
SNAP SHACKLE – Shackle with a secure locking mechanism instead of a pin.
SPAR – General term for a mast, boom, gaff or pole.
SPONSON – Inflatable tube around a RIB or inflatable dinghy.
SPREADER – A strut usually fitted in pairs to deflect the shrouds and control the bending characteristics of the mast.
SPRING TIDE – Extreme high tide caused by the gravitational pull of the moon.

SQUALL – Sudden, short-lived increase in wind.

STANCHION – Vertical pole supporting guard rails.

STANDING RIGGING – Fixed rigging.

STAND-ON-BOAT – Right of way boat.

STARBOARD – Right hand side of the boat.

STAY – Forward mast support.

STEM – Forward extremity of the boat.

STEPPED HULL – Right angle step in the bottom of a planing hull designed to suck air into the boundary layer and reduce skin friction.

STERN – Aft extremity of the boat.

STERN GLAND – Prop shaft seal to stop water ingress within the hull.

STOPPER – A cleating device that holds a sheet or halyard fast.

STROP – A ring of rope or wire used to make up an attachment to a spar.

SWAGE – Pressed wire terminal.

SWIVEL – Connector whose two parts rotate.

SWIVEL BLOCK – Block with a swivel joint.

T

TABERNACLE – Structure supporting a deck-stepped mast.

TACKLE – Multi-purchase system.

TAIL – The free end of a sheet or halyard.

TALURIT – Swaged wire splice.

THWART – Transverse seat or plank amidships.

TIDAL STREAM – Flow of water caused by the rise and fall of tide.

TIDE – Six-hourly rise and fall of water caused by the gravitational pull of the moon.

TILLER – Arm of a rudder to control boat direction.

TRAILING EDGE – Aft edge of a foil, i.e. sail, keel, rudder, etc.

TRANSIT – Sighting two objects in line.

TRANSOM – Transverse aft end of a boat.

TRAVELLER – Fitting on a rope or track with limited travel used to adjust the mainsheet.

TRIM TAB – Adjustable elevator to adjust the boat's fore and aft when running.

TRIMARAN – Three-hulled multihull.

TRUCKER'S HITCH – Knot to tension a tie rope.

TRUE WIND – Direction and velocity of wind measured at a stationary position.

TUGMAN'S HITCH – Knot to secure towing strop to winch.

V

V-HULL – Deep V hull with a deadrise of 18–25°.

VARIATION – Difference in angle between True North and Magnetic North.

VENTED HULL – See stepped hull.

VMG – Velocity made good to windward.

W

WAKE – Turbulence left astern of a moving boat.

WARP – Rope used to moor a boat.

WEATHER SHORE – Shoreline where the wind is blowing offshore.

WETTED SURFACE – Total underwater area of the hull.

WINCH – Capstan used to wind in an anchor cable.

WINDAGE – Drag caused by the boat and crew.

WINDWARD – Towards the wind; opposite of leeward.

WINDLASS – See Winch.

WORKING END – End of a rope used to tie a knot.

Index

Acknowledgements

Our thanks go to surveyor Adrian White MIIMS, and John Kilhams from the International Institute of Marine Surveying for their invaluable advice and support during the production of this book. Other valuable contributions have come from Beneteau, Bertram Yachts, Chaparral Powerboats, Craig Loomes, Edgewater Powerboats, Evinrude outboards, Fletcher Boats, Glacier Bay, Grand Banks, Honda outboards, Jeanneau, Johnson outboards, Orkney Boats, Peter Freebody & Co, Ribcraft, Seafox, Sealine International, Seaward Boats, Shetland Boats, Triumph Boats, Volvo Penta and Wally Yachts.

Our appreciation also goes to the following manufacturers,for providing information and photographs: Harry Arnold/PPL: 48, 58 Peter Bentley/PPL: 68 Bertram Yacht Inc: 18 Cobia Boat Company: 11 Greg Collins/PPL: 113, 130 Graham Franks/PPL: 46 Peter Freebody & Co: 24 Bob Grieser/PPL: 119 Robert Holland Dougherty: 55 Forest Johnson: 19 Gilles Martin-Raget: 66 Magnus Pajnerj: 2, 42, 74 Mark Pepper/PPL: 14 Barry Pickthall/PPL: 41, 52, 60-61, 79, 89, 91, 92, 93, 95, 96, 97, 99, 100, 101, 103, 104, 105, 121, 124 PPL: 19, 42, 52-53 Keith Pritchard/PPL: 31 Eileen Ramsay/PPL: 48 K J Richardon/PPL: 12 Sea Angler: 52-53 Triumph Boats: 10.

Grateful thanks must also go to PPL's designers Kayleigh Reynolds and George Gray and to Andrew Wetherall and the picture research team at PPL Photo Agency for sourcing the many photographs we needed to illustrate particular points throughout this book.

Design and illustrations: Kayleigh Reynolds and George Gray.

Photo research: PPL Photo Agency.

Photography: PPL Photo Agency.